ALTERNATIVE FUTURES FOR WORSHIP
Anointing of the Sick

ALTERNATIVE FUTURES FOR WORSHIP

Volume 7
Anointing of the Sick

Volume Editor

PETER E. FINK, S.J.

Authors

ORLO STRUNK, JR.
JENNIFER GLEN, C.C.V.I.
WALTER H. CUENIN
GERALD CALHOUN, S.J.
PETER E. FINK, S.J.
MARY FRANCES DUFFY, G.N.S.H.

THE LITURGICAL PRESS
Collegeville, Minnesota 56321

ISBN 0-8146-1499-X

1   2   3   4   5   6   7   8

Library of Congress Cataloging-in-Publication Data
Alternative futures for worship.

Includes bibliographies.
Contents: v. 1. General Introduction / volume editor, Regis A. Duffy ; authors, Michael A. Cowan, Paul J. Philibert, Edward J. Kilmartin — v. 2. Baptism and confirmation / edited by Mark Searle ; by Andrew D. Thompson . . . [et al.] — v. 3. The eucharist / edited by Bernard J. Lee ; by Thomas Richstatter . . . [et al.] — [etc.]

1. Sacraments (Liturgy) 2. Catholic Church—Liturgy.
I. Lee, Bernard J., 1932–
BX2200.A49   1987   265   86-27300
ISBN 0-8146-1491-4 (set)

CONTENTS

THE CONTRIBUTORS

ORLO STRUNK, JR. is professor emeritus, Boston University, the managing editor of *The Journal of Pastoral Care*, and a pastoral psychotherapist in The Grand Strand Pastoral Counseling Service in Myrtle Beach, South Carolina.

JENNIFER GLEN, C.C.V.I., teaches liturgy at the University of St. Thomas School of Theology (St. Mary's Seminary Campus) in Houston.

WALTER H. CUENIN is associate pastor of Sacred Heart Church in Lexington, Massachusetts, and adjunct associate professor of sacraments and liturgy at the Weston School of Theology.

GERALD CALHOUN, S.J., is a former director of the clinical-pastoral program at Youville Hospital in Cambridge, Massachusetts, and is the director of novices for the New England Province of the Society of Jesus.

PETER E. FINK, S.J., is associate professor of liturgical theology at the Weston School of Theology and has been a frequent contributor to *Worship* and other professional journals.

MARY FRANCES DUFFY, G.N.S.H., a member of the Grey Nuns of the Sacred Heart, is a liturgist and pastoral counselor serving in the department of pastoral care, Good Samaritan Hospital in Baltimore.

PREFACE

Alternative Futures for Worship is not a product. It is rather a window through which a relationship may be observed. Or to change the image, it is a listening device with which a conversation may be overheard. The participants are sacramental theology, liturgical experience, and the human sciences.

All of life—like all the world—has the possibility of mediating the transformative encounter between God and human history. That is its sacramental character. In the Roman Catholic tradition there has evolved over a long history a system of seven sacraments. These are not our only sacramental experiences. But they occupy a privileged sacramental role in the life of this Christian community.

Each sacrament concerns itself with the religious meanings of some important slice of human life. There are not many slices of life whose patterns and interpreted meanings have not been probed and described by the human sciences. It is crucial, therefore, that sacramental and liturgical theology pay very careful attention indeed to the deliverances of the human sciences. Religious experience cannot, of course, be reduced to the descriptive reports of the human sciences. Yet it would be foolhardy to theologize or "liturgize" apart from serious consideration of these many empirical attempts to understand the character of lived experience in our culture and our time.

Each volume in this series exemplifies the processes of encounter between sacrament, liturgy, and the human sciences: what reports from the human sciences are being considered; how do these understandings affect the meaning structure of the sacrament; how would these meanings find liturgical expression. Every volume in the series has this fundamental agenda, but each takes it up in its own particular way. Our aims are modest; we have not intended to produce any exactly right conclusion. We only care to engage in serious, imaginative, and highly responsible conversation.

It may seem that proposing alternative sacramental rituals is irresponsible, and it would be if they were proposed for anyone's actual use. They are not! This is not an underground sacramentary. We are most aware of the tentative and groping character of each of these attempts.

However, we believe with William James that the best way to understand what something means (like this conversation between Christian experience and the human sciences) is to see what difference it makes. James says you must set an idea to work in the stream of experience to know what it means. We choose ritual as that stream of experience.

Sacramental rituals are not themselves the sacraments. The sacraments are temporally thick slices of life which through time mediate religious experience. The liturgical rite is but one moment in this thicker-than-rite sacramentalization of life. It is a privileged moment though. Ritual is a moment of high value if it illuminates and intensifies the meaning of sacrament. Leonard Bernstein's "Mass for Theatre" speaks movingly of the absurdity of ritual when it has lost touch with the lives of the people who are supposed to be celebrating it. When private meanings and public ritual meanings do not intersect (which is not to say coincide), the absurdity is thundering.

Because a ritual puts a sacramental understanding under the spotlight, we have elected to explore the conversation between sacramental life and the human sciences by imagining ritual appropriations of the fruits of the conversation. That is our way of setting an idea to work imaginatively in the stream of experience. That, and nothing more! But that is a lot.

We suggest that any readers of this volume who have not done so read the introductory volume. There we have tried to say more fully what we think we are about in this entire series and why the many authors who contributed to it are convinced that this project is a quite right thing to do. We are happy to have you listen in on our conversation. Our long-term hope is that you may join it.

Bernard J. Lee, S.M.
San Antonio, Texas

INTRODUCTION

Peter E. Fink, S.J.

Among the most appealing traits of Jesus as he is portrayed in the New Testament is the care and concern he exhibited toward those who were sick. Healing stories abound and tell of a Jesus who is gentle, moved with compassion, and eager to touch and make well those who approach him in faith. The healing ministry of Jesus is given as central to his proclamation of the kingdom of God and is cited on at least two occasions as a primary witness to the fact that in him the kingdom of God has come. To the seventy-two who are sent on before him, he says, "heal the sick and say to them, 'The kingdom of God has come near to you'" (Luke 10:9), and to the question put to him by the disciples of John the Baptist he replies, "Go and tell John what you have seen and heard: the blind receive their sight, the lame walk, lepers are cleansed, and the deaf hear, the dead are raised up, the poor have good news preached to them" (Luke 7:22). In the healing of the sick, Jesus gives bold witness to the power and the presence of the kingdom of God.

From its earliest days the Church has known itself to be a community of men and women commissioned by Christ to proclaim his Word and continue in their lives his own saving work. For this he goes to the Father, that "whoever believes in me will do the works that I do, and even greater" (John 14:12). For this, too, he remains in the midst of his Church, the fountain and source of all we are able to do.

Among the works entrusted to the Church is this same care and concern for the sick that was so evident in Jesus' earthly ministry.

And his ministry to the sick did indeed continue, as is amply borne witness to by the many healing stories recounted in the Acts of the Apostles. One need only recall the charming story of Peter healing the lame beggar at the Beautiful Gate (Acts 3:1-6), or the healings attributed to Philip at Samaria (Acts 8:4ff.), or again Peter at Lydda and Joppa curing a lame man and raising Tabitha from the dead (Acts 10:32-43). Not only was the healing ministry of Christ passed on to his community of disciples, but Christ's own power to heal was given to those who believe.

This volume of *Alternative Futures for Worship* is dedicated to the healing ministry of Christ as it is expressed and embodied in the sacrament of the anointing of the sick. The time frame is the second half of the twentieth century, and the projection of the volume is forward. Yet the ministry itself and the sacrament which is in focus have been vital and vibrant forces throughout the history of the Church. It is true, as Walter Cuenin notes in his brief historical sketch, that the shapes and forms of this sacramental ministry have not always been clear or well-targeted. Nonetheless the healing of the sick has remained a central concern of the Church from its very beginning.

The reforms of the Second Vatican Council have gone a long way to restoring this sacrament as the sacrament of the sick, reversing a history that had seen it relegated to the seriously ill and those on the verge of death. The section of the *Roman Ritual* entitled "Pastoral Care of the Sick: Rites of Anointing and Viaticum" locates the sacramental act within the larger context of pastoral care and presents a wide variety of prayers and scripture texts to be used on visits to the sick, at communion for the sick, for the actual anointing of the sick, within Mass and outside of Mass, in praying for an individual in the midst of his or her family and caregivers, or praying for many gathered in liturgical assembly. It also gives rites and prayers for the dying, likewise located within the larger context of pastoral care. Viaticum is restored as *the* sacrament of the dying, and in addition to its celebration prayers of commendation are given for the dying, those who have died, and, as must be included, for the families and friends of those who have died. In all "Pastoral Care of the Sick" is a remarkably successful liturgical text that cannot help but serve well both those who walk the painful journey through sickness and in many cases toward death, as well as those who walk the journey with them.

Why then this book of alternative futures? It is certainly not intended to slight the achievement of the revised *Roman Ritual,* nor indeed to suggest that "Pastoral Care of the Sick" ought to be bypassed. On the contrary, the rituals in this volume grow very much out of the same spirit which has already produced so many fine ritual texts and wishes perhaps only to stretch work already done in further directions which are suggested by, but not always followed through in, these new rites for anointing and viaticum.

The point of departure for this volume, as it is for each volume in the *Alternative Futures* series, is a contribution from the human sciences. The question put to Orlo Strunk was simply this: are there any challenges that the human sciences might make to those who would generate and use rituals of healing? His answer, drawn from his long experience as professor, pastor, and clinician, is clearly designed to complement and locate the current ritual offerings of the Church. His remarks call attention to the need to relate both *text,* that is, the individual who is being ministered to, and *context,* the larger community arena in which the ministry takes place.

The rituals offered in "Pastoral Care of the Sick" do indeed allow for adaptation to the uniqueness of each individual being ministered to, though, because they focus so much on the individual who is sick, they do not address in any strong way the question of context, that is, the family, the helpers, and the larger Christian community, all of whom are likewise implicated in the illness at hand. So Strunk's challenge is both *to* the current rituals, insofar as they need to be adapted to the uniqueness of the individual who is sick for their proper enactment, and *beyond* these rituals into arenas of pastoral care that have yet to be addressed.

The same may be said of Jennifer Glen's careful reflection on the pastoral theology of anointing. While holding herself in dialogue with Strunk's reflections and offering a complementary phenomenological assessment of the experience of being sick, her main point is to explore the depths of the "reign of God" as a source of eschatological faith and as a resource for healing on a level that may include but is deeper than bodily healing. This she suggests both for those who are sick, those in attendance on the sick, and indeed all in the community of the Church.

Walter Cuenin's historical sketch not only recalls the main threads of the history of the sacrament, but also notes some areas of the Church's life that, while larger than the sacrament, nonetheless are manifestations of the healing ministry of Christ in the

Church. He also draws from that history several key issues which ritual work for the future ought to consider in some way or other.

The first alternative future, presented by Gerald Calhoun, is in many ways neither alternative nor future. It is primarily a pastoral essay giving what might be called the "inners" of both current and future ritual texts. A specific group is targeted, namely the long-term seriously ill, and what the chapter illustrates is the care that must go into deciding what ritual should be employed and how it should be enacted. Glen noted in her chapter that many of the issues of text raised by Strunk can not be built into the ritual text as written, but need to be added by the minister or ministers in translating ritual text into ritual prayer. Calhoun's reflections are prior to ritual and are needed as the ritual forms to be employed gradually take shape. I have appended to his chapter a sample ritual using mainly materials from "Pastoral Care of the Sick" to illustrate how this pastoral sensitivity may take shape in ritual form.

The two rituals offered by Mary Frances Duffy do take the imagination well beyond the current ritual texts and this in two different ways. Her first seeks to address the needs of those who are in attendance on the sick, namely, family, friends, and primary caregivers. It recognizes that these all too often fall through the cracks while attention is rightly given to the sick. Yet these are affected by the sickness of another and in need of some attention themselves. Duffy's first ritual is a healing ritual for those satellite persons who are in need of some healing if they are to properly minister in faith to the sick.

Her second ritual seeks to focus on a nonphysical yet definitely tangible form of dissolution of meaning that parallels in its contours the experience of sickness. This is the now well-described mid-life crisis, which hits people anywhere between the ages of thirty-five and fifty-five. This is an example of ritual extension by analogy. Even for the healthy mid-life seems to evoke levels of experience similar to those evoked by sickness, and Duffy is convinced that a ritual of healing is not inappropriate to address such analogous experience. Though she focuses primarily on the experience of mid-life, she invites the readers to extend the analogy even further to other nonphysical experiences of dissolution.

The final ritual is of another sort altogether. As its introduction claims, it is an untroubled ritual for untroubled times, and its primary aim is to provide context for the enactment of the sacrament in time of sickness. Without such context the anointing of the sick can seem to come from nowhere, without richness of nuance to enhance its healing power. The aim of this last ritual is to locate the truth of healing squarely within the ordinary prayer life of the community, "lest we forget." For this the popular tradition of the throat blessing on the feast of St. Blaise is extended in meaning and scope and located in the midst of the ordinary fare of Ordinary Time.

There are no illusions in this work that what we present here is exhaustive. The issues are plain. Our suggestions are samples to serve Christ's healing power and care in the face of those issues. Other ritual extensions need also to be imagined. These we must leave to others. If these which we do offer serve to stimulate the imagination further, to aid in the careful employment of those rituals given in "Pastoral Care of the Sick," and to assist in the genesis of new rituals that may take Christ's healing even further into the lives of people, then we will have succeeded in our deepest hopes.

Weston School of Theology
Cambridge, Massachusetts

1. THE HUMAN SCIENCES AND THE EXPERIENCES OF DIMINISHMENT AND DISSOLUTION

Orlo Strunk, Jr.

Although there is nothing new in the Church's desire for a wise cultural adaptation of its liturgies, the present times appear to offer challenges never before experienced by humankind. In the last several decades consciousness-raising and technological leaps have been staggering. The advent of television and microcomputers alone have extended the potential for consciousness-expansion beyond the most delirious imaginations of previous decades. This new load—or "overload"—of information is truly amazing, and adaptation to these overloads has become for many a project of gigantic proportion.

The health care milieu is only one in which technology has reached a point beyond the dreams of most of us, but it is a crucial one. Laser beams, microsurgery, genetic manipulation, CAT scanners, and pharmaceutical innovations constitute a major part of the contemporary health care scene. In all of this, as John Naisbitt has dramatically depicted in his *Megatrends*, we need somehow to discover a balance between high technology and high touch. It seems evident that there is an inevitable tendency for high technology to lead to a distancing between patient and healers. Machines and techniques have a way of standing between persons.

Strange as it may seem, religious rituals do not always escape this technological propensity. Who among us has not been the recipient of a rite delivered in a cold, impersonal, and starkly mundane fashion? High tech projects, like any other ideological movement, have cannibalistic tendencies. The massive and conspicuous successes of science and technology tend to make such tendencies both intense and laudable. They tend therefore to color *all* of life, including religion and its modes of addressing self and world.

But blind resistance is not the creative response of the mature religious project. Instead, religious institutions are called to discover new ways of integrating authentic technology—to own, in a manner of speaking, the new discoveries and to find ways of embracing the new within the wisdom of the old.

Admittedly, this is no easy task.

In this chapter, a few ideas for the understanding of this task will be presented, ideas which reflect only one small facet of the science technology zeitgeist, the human sciences.

At first this may seem strange—turning to science for assistance in adapting to contexts created, partly at least, by its own constructions. After all, it could be argued, it is the behavioral and social sciences which most threaten the religious project. As a student of mine recently put it, "Psychology *is* the religion of our day!"

But that is to take an adversarial stance and to continue the age-old war between science and religion. Rather, the Church in its compassion and comprehension is called to embrace and to learn from *every* source of knowledge.

Thus it is that within the behavioral and social sciences themselves are perspectives, processes, and findings which might prove helpful in liturgical adaptations, specifically in this instance in a ritual of healing. The overarching question is then: *what processes and knowledge need to be taken into account by anyone who would seek to develop this ritual in today's world?*

In attempting to answer this question, I hope to take very seriously the text/context metaphor, which itself is becoming something of a paradigm for a wide range of fields of inquiry, including those often contained within the behavioral social science rubric.

For those in the Christian tradition, particularly those who wish to understand biblical messages within the historic epoch in which they were originally composed, this text/context notion will not be a new one. But it has been somewhat difficult for the behavioral/social sciences to come to terms with the need to see persons (texts) and cultures (contexts) as interactional and always interrelated. The tendency to analyze—a very strong tendency in the sciences—often has lead to treatment in depth of one or the other of these complex galaxies, but not in terms of their imbedded characteristics.

Starting with Experience

We should not be surprised to learn that despite the many accomplishments of modern science—including those forms called behavioral, social, and human—there are serious dissatisfactions being heard from within. The liturgist wishing to take into account the findings of psychology and sociology, for instance, would do well to recognize from the start that not all is well within these disciplines, despite their current status and prestige in our culture. Although it is not the purpose of this chapter to catalogue the critics' arguments relative to the current state of affairs in the human sciences, there is one observation which is so crucial to the task of this fascicle that it needs to be noted and explicated a bit. It is what might be called the "phenomenological reminder."

Often it is argued that theology strays far from human experience. It is frequently a criticism cast at the theological task by both those from the outside as well as those from the inside of that project. Theology is abstract; theology is obtuse; theology is irrelevant—thus goes the argument. What is often implied in these criticisms is that other fields of inquiry do not stray in this way. After all psychology—as an example—is preoccupied with the personal equation and with the experiencing organism!

But this simply is not so. The behavioral and social sciences are not ipso facto immune to such distancing tendencies. Indeed the elaborate theoretical systems designed to give intelligible form to the complexities of the human psyche and to human relationships often become distal and foreign to the realities of a lived world. Thus it is that in the current critique of even the behavioral and social sciences, we find the phenomenological reminder, the prompting, that remaining close to experience and to its description is a necessary preparatory discipline. In terms of the metaphor mentioned in the beginning of this chapter, the *text* (person) dare not be lost in an enthusiasm to understand the *context* (such as theories, structures, situations, and cultures). Authentic meaning is only achieved when text and context are taken seriously in their connectedness and in their imbeddedness.

What does this mean for the liturgist desirous of facilitating a sacrament focused on the sick? It seems to me that there are at least three questions called into consideration and in need of reflection:

1. *What is being sick like for me?*

As we shall see, there are some firm generalizations designed to answer this question, and it is important for the liturgist and all caregivers to know about these general answers. But the personal experience of being ill requires a personal consideration and reflection. Reconstructing and describing that experience may or may not correlate well with the general answers.

Although I have rarely been seriously ill in my lifetime, on those few occasions when I have been ill, I have felt a deep melancholy flood my being. I want nothing more than to be let alone to draw on my own inner resources and to find comfort in solitude. My thoughts return to my childhood and in vivid imagery I romp the fields, hills, and swamps of eastern Pennsylvania. I withdraw into a world of recollected images, content to walk about in a rich universe of experiences, events, and ideas that are peculiarly *mine.*

My spouse, on the other hand, experiences illness quite another way. She reports a pervasive sense of fear and frustration, and her need for others, especially her family, is deeply felt. Unless she is desperately sick, which she has been on several occasions, she yearns for others to be around her. She feels better when she is making contact with other persons.

These two simple sketches illustrate how texts differ. If either of us showed wonder about the nature of a liturgy focused on helping a person find peace and some acceptance in illness, we would wonder *differently.* True there are commonalities in our being ill, but there are important differences as well. To be aware of this personal equation may help us to be sensitive to the power and the reality of the text, a sensitization essential when text and context meet to create meaning.

2. *What is being ministered to like for me?*

The person who wishes to develop a ritual of care and support needs to recall and reflect on what it feels like to have a rite become part of his or her situation. Is it a frightening experience? Does it feel intrusive? Does it create relief, reduce fear, calm the soul? What is there about the ministration that seems to create the feelings and/or thoughts?

There is no single answer to questions such as these. Such phenomenological kinds of knowledge will vary greatly, and if we are honest in our reflections and if we listen carefully to the accounts shared with us by others, we will come to appreciate the reality of variability and not be captured by the tyrannical power of commonality and generalization which constantly pulls us towards a surety and comfort which do an injustice to the text, the suffering person.

A special warning needs to be heard at this point. The lure of developmental and phase theories can be misleading, as important as they are. Although stages of dying made explicit in the works of Elisabeth Kübler-Ross, for instance, are helpful and invaluable in understanding this process, our common thirst for closure can lead us to convert such guidelines into dogma, usually to the detriment of those to whom we minister, not to mention the harm involved in not fully appreciating the complexity of God's creation.

3. *How does getting well feel for me?*

What can we recall about that process—perhaps an excruciatingly slow one—which returns us to what we have come to regard as our normal state of health? Are we impatient with the healing movement? What are the tones of our prayers, our conversations with others, and our communications with physicians, nurses, chaplains, and attendants? Here is what one woman recalls about recovering from a ruptured appendix:

> I remember waking up very early in the morning and for the first time in a week asking for a mirror. Up to that time I hadn't really cared how I looked; the pain and discomfort had clouded my mind. I wanted only sleep and the drugs that led me away from the pain. But on that morning when I asked to see myself in a mirror, I began to get well. I felt something different going on inside me. I still had pain and I cried alot, but I knew that I was at last getting well.

What is important about such phenomenological reports is that they alert us to the personal equation and assist us in holding to a realistic expectation in regard to any rite designed to offer promise and hope. As we shall note, if the empirical demonstrations of the human sciences can contribute anything to liturgical projects, it is that it is only when the full complexity and idiosyncrasies of both text and context are appreciated and taken into account that authentic meaning takes place.

Psychosocial Factors of Illness

The sciences, including the behavioral and social sciences, always thirst after generalizations. At the same time sciences such as psychology and psychiatry need to deal with the individual. It is this point-counterpoint dynamic which generates the complexities and ambiguities frequently found in the human sciences. As social psychologists and anthropologists are fond of reminding us, every person is in certain respects like all other persons, like some other persons, and like no other person.

The liturgist faces the grand challenge of appreciating these realities in the attempt to communicate meaning. At some point he or she may be helped by appraising some of the psychosocial factors which have been noticed and empirically studied by the human sciences. The following listing of such factors is in no sense exhaustive; it is meant to suggest how multifarious is the "text" which is exposed to a rite designed for the sick.

Natural Narcissism

Although in the psychiatric and psychological literature the narcissistic personality is considered a disorder in which there is a grandiose sense of self-importance or uniqueness, there is what might be called a natural narcissism in all of us. It is a given, having extreme importance in thinking about a person who has fallen ill. In early psychoanalytic theory the so-called "narcissistic type" was considered to be a psychological type in which the chief interest is focused on self-preservation. Who among us would not come into this category to at least one degree or another?

What falling ill does is attack or wound this narcissistic sense. The stronger the narcissistic trait the greater will be the repercussions. We have all entertained the quiet conviction that a serious illness would not come to us. *Others* may get cancer; not us. Although the self-importance and the uniqueness factors may be only mild and not deserving the psychiatric designation of narcissistic, the sense is there, and when taken ill, the threat to this evaluation of ourselves is assaulted. Reactions then become a part of the "text."

Common Reactions to Falling Ill

When illness strikes, persons respond in amazingly complex ways. Anger is a very common response, and its direction and expression are determined by many personality and environmental forces. For some persons the anger remains unexpressed and is transformed into depression or a pervasive sadness. Of course frustration is frequently a dominant reaction, particularly when the illness greatly limits mobility.

The by now famous framework identified by Elisabeth Kübler-Ross—denial, anger, bargaining, depression, and acceptance—in regard to the dying person can be helpful in appreciating the many feelings involved in the terminally ill person, particularly if they are seen not as sequential phases but as *feelings which come and go, rise and fall, merge and emerge.* For the fact is that each person's dying, like each person's illness, is as unique as each person's living.

It is probably safe to say that there is hardly an emotion that cannot be triggered by an illness. Thus it is that the person becomes an exaggerated "text" during such periods.

Personality Factors Determining Reactions

Despite our general theories of response and development, all of which contribute to a reading of the text, variations and deviations are many. Some of these can be accounted for in terms of personality variables. The introvert, for example, may handle illness quite differently than an extrovert. The introvert as a type directs psychic energy toward self, whereas the extrovert tends to move toward external nature and social phenomena. Even within these two general types are significant nuances helping to account for a person's reaction to illness.

Or consider the qualities of attribution associated with personality. Research reveals that individuals fall on a continuum in terms of assigning cause to events. At one end is the person who consistently views conditions as arising beyond the self, centered in some force external to one's personal sense. At the other end is the individual who attributes causes to an inner world where personal responsibility assumes a major role in one's life and in one's understanding. Obviously such propensities will play themselves out in the midst of an illness.

Perhaps even more startling are the initial findings related to the temporal dimensions of consciousness, the so-called right-brain/left-brain research. Although popularization has tended to oversimplify the research into hemispheric functions, it appears certain that modes of consciousness may partly be traceable to these brain factors. The left hemisphere is predominantly involved with analytical, logical thinking, primarily linear in operation, whereas the right hemisphere specializes in holistic mentation, with an orientation that is much more relational in nature. As yet this massive body of literature has not been integrated into the operations of worship and ritual, but surely it holds promise in helping us to get a better reading of human ways of being and responding to liturgies of all kinds.

In the 1960s, for example, the cry for right brain modes of "doing a liturgy" illustrated the lopsided orientation of much worship and ritual. On one occasion I recall entering the seminary chapel and discovering colorful balloons and cardboard pie plates hanging from the rafters. Students carried other students about and over the pews, and the music was strange and different. We (the faculty) thought the circus atmosphere antithetical to true worship. Our problem then as now had to do with finding authentic ways of integrating right and left brain propensities in creative ways.

Even this cursory and highly selective notation of psychosocial factors provides at least a hint into the recent discoveries coming from the personality sciences. If we think of personality as the dynamic mutual interaction of all systems which comprise and affect the organism, we realize how important the personality sciences can be in coming to an appreciation of text. These systems will include what we commonly call the physical, social, economic, political, ecological, and spiritual. Given such a complexity, an element of mystery always abounds. Perhaps what Norman Cousins in his *Anatomy of an Illness as Perceived by the Patient* calls "the chemistry of the will to live" encompasses this intricate grouping of "systems."

But there is much more beyond what may be thought of as personality factors.

The Reality of Idiosyncratic Factors

The more systemic the human sciences have become, the more they have had to account for variations in generalizations and the more they have had to contextualize such general "truths." Indeed one of the most challenging projects facing the contemporary human sciences is finding ways of *including* factors previously overlooked, denied, or minimized. The following sample of such factors illustrates the new challenge, at the same time suggesting that text and context may be far more complex than previously considered.

GENDER

Contemporary research and theory in the behavioral and social sciences must now take very seriously the gender factor. In the past a great number of psychological and psychiatric theories, for instance, were constructed using a male-dominated model. As we have come to realize, theories in the human sciences are as much a reflection of the wider culture as they are of scientific discoveries.

What this means is that future research, as well as the utilizations of findings from past studies, must be viewed critically. To suppose, for example, that illness is experienced the same way by men as by women cannot be accepted as a truism. Instead, the gender factor becomes a part of the "text," offering new challenges to the applied social scientist as well as to those wishing to utilize human science data in nonscientific projects.

ETHNICITY

The power of an individual's ethnic background impacts understanding and contributes to the complexity of "text." Again the tendency has been to consider, either consciously or unconsciously, that white male middle class factors are normative and to construct generalizations from this image. Often in noting America as a melting pot, overgeneralizations have led to oversimplifications. The ways in which Irish-Americans in South Boston view hospital admissions, for instance, may vary considerably from those of German descent living in Eastern Pennsylvania—not to mention differences when considering the Amish living in the very same geographical region. Nor do Azorians living in southern New England view the characteristics of "mental health" the same way as does the white midwesterner mental health professional who has been trained in an Eastern university.

Although recent accomplishments in recognizing ethnic differences have been advanced in terms of blacks, the power of such factors as related to other ethnic groups is only beginning to become part of the human sciences' search for understanding. The liturgist who wishes to discover the most efficacious fit regarding text and context overlooks such variables at a serious cost in meaning.

DEVELOPMENT

For the past decade developmental principles have taken a central place in theory and research in the human sciences, particularly in the fields of psychology and psychiatry. Although the seminal work of Jean Piaget took a long time to find its way into the mainstream of American behavioral and social sciences, when its impact came it stimulated an amazing assortment of developmental perspectives; for example, the moral development theories and research of Lawrence Kohlberg and the faith development works of James Fowler. All such approaches take place within a broad developmental principle which claims that psychosocial understandings must take seriously stages or phases where an individual is when a particular event, such as illness, takes place.

Although these developmental theories and research findings have found their way into religious institutions, particularly in the areas of religious education and pastoral care, their values have not been fully realized in actual liturgical practices. It may be that the self-evident quality of the developmental principles may cause us at times to overlook the power of such factors. Nevertheless they do hold great potential for reshaping liturgical practices and in developing rites for a variety of life's passages.

Systemic Factors

What is characterizing contemporary human sciences more and more is the growing sensitivities to the variety of systems which need to be recognized in any truly authentic attempt to comprehend the relationship between self and world. Perspectives such as world views, personal metaphors, and cosmological views are becoming increasingly evident as important variables in seeing more clearly the text/context dynamics. All hold potential for understanding how persons respond to suffering and to those operations suggestive of healing and wellness.

WORLD VIEW

Within the past two decades the notion of world view has begun to assume greater and greater importance in the human sciences. Eclipsed for a time by psychoanalysis with its emphasis on the unconscious and by behaviorism with its preoccupation with overt acts, the emergence—or reemergence—of cognitive approaches has revitalized an interest in the ways in which persons and even nations construct the world. Studies in the content and organization of value systems, for instance, have alerted the sociologist and the social psychologist to the influence of moral factors on individual and group behavior.

Over twenty years ago Florence Kluckholn and Fred Strodtbeck, American anthropologists, proposed that the structure of social communities is founded on "value orientations" designed to answer five common human problems: what is the basic nature of humankind?

(good, evil, mixed, neither); what will be humankind's relationship to nature? (subjugation to, harmony with, mastery over); what is the preferred focus in time? (past, present, future); what will be the orientation toward activity? (doing, being, being-in-becoming); and what will be people's relationship to people? (lineal, collateral, individualistic). Although such a schema has been critiqued and many others proposed, the notion that there are such broad, guiding projects which help to account for specific behavior is being taken seriously by more and more contemporary behavioral and social scientists.

The Harvard psychologist Gordon W. Allport once listed the various aspects of growth significant in the development of personality, starting with simple differentiations and ending with the personal *Weltanschauung.* He wrote: "As soon as an individual's philosophy of life is known, his personal activities, which taken by themselves are meaningless, become understood." This suggests that a person's world view becomes important when he or she becomes ill, and their responses to illness, and to those healing acts that may follow, partly will be conditioned by *Weltanschauung.*

Equally illustrative of this variable is Adrian van Kaam's notion of projects of existence. This priest-psychologist, who has done so much to translate into American psychology and religious life the insights of psychological existentialism, defines a project of existence as "the hidden design, the inner orientation which makes us realize our existence in a personal way . . . our conscious or partly conscious plan of living our individual lives."

Whatever concept we may find helpful, the general conception coming from the human sciences is that molar notions contribute to an attempt to comprehend the "text." What may be of particular importance to the liturgist is not simply how this factor leads to a better understanding of text, but in what ways a ritual serves the person when her or his world view is being threatened or fragmented by an enemy called illness.

Personal Metaphors

In recent years psychotherapy has moved far beyond its original stance of psychoanalysis. Although psychodynamic-oriented psychotherapy remains a dominant theory and practice, many newer therapies have been developed within the past several decades. Just as traditional psychotherapies hold significant implications for the religionist, including the liturgist, so too do those current psychotherapeutic modes stemming from humanistic-existential theories and practices. One example is the growing recognition that metaphor is a helpful concept in the understanding of persons and in providing help to persons.

Literary figures, particularly poets, have for centuries appreciated the power of the metaphor in capturing and making form from a swirl of meaningless factors.

A metaphor describes—usually in terms of something else—some thing, event, or person that if described in literal terms would require more language and explanation. What psychotherapists are learning is that individuals may be understood in terms of dominant metaphors, that a client's traits and experiences and associations often can be formed and codified once the personal metaphor is discovered. The woman whose past can be captured in the phrase "she's a princess" is quite different from another who has come to see herself as "the tiger in the family." Undoubtedly the responses of a princess and a tiger will vary considerably as they meet the events of life.

FAMILY SYSTEMS THEORY

The advent of family therapy represents a revolution in the psychotherapeutic community. In one sense it is an expression of systems theories in the wider behavioral science movement. General systems theory, partly in reaction to more mechanical cybernetic theories and to individualistic models of behavior, is based on the conviction that living organisms are organized wholes and not just the sum of their parts and that they are essentially open systems, maintaining themselves with continuous inputs from and outputs to the environment. This way of thinking—a new metaphor of a sort—revolutionized the way family therapy has developed.

This more systemic way of thinking, of course, holds implications far beyond family therapy itself. Pastoral care for those who are sick or dying, for instance, has found that it needs to widen its vision to include working with the families as well as the "identified patient." If a faithful celebration of a sacrament is seen as a goal and occasion for this pastoral care, many healings may result beyond the identified patient. Pastoral care, when envisioned systemically, may assist in dealing with much unfinished business such as the reconciling of estranged family members and helping to reduce anxiety and fear about those who are left behind after a death. The notion that illness touches many lives beyond the individual sufferer has many consequences for pastoral care, including that part of it we have come to call "liturgical."

Systems theory, particularly as it has evolved in an understanding of family dynamics, poses a real challenge for anyone wishing to formulate religious rites which can be functional and at the same time lift up promises of hope.

COSMOLOGICAL VIEWS

At one time the behavioral and social science researchers considered cosmological perspectives to be too distal to behavior to warrant serious study, but with the reemergence of cognitive psychology has come a renewed interest in the nature of cosmologies and the ways in which they help to account for perceptions, attitudes, values, experience, and behavior. Sometimes the recognition takes the form of seeing a cosmology as a reflection of self-definition, thus suggesting that cosmologies are in fact anthropologies. The idea is that humans must construct the cosmos through their own biological and cultural equipment and propensities.

At the same time commonalities of cosmologies are identified and named. An example would be a classification which sees humans as orthodox, or existential, or evolutionary, or psychological. Such views are the natural content for explorations in ancient philosophies and theologies, but behavioral scientists focus a bit differently than speculative scholars of the past. They tend to be more interested in discovering how cosmologies are made manifest in real life situations.

What may be of particular importance for the liturgist is sensitivity to the reality that new cosmologies are in our midst and that these new views carry with them both losses and gains.

It does appear that the cosmology of classical science is crumbling and that a new cosmology is slowly forming in human consciousness. Contemporary developments in modern physics, for example, have opened up a new understanding of the universe; it is no longer seen as a collection of physical objects but as an interconnected system within a unified whole. Relativity theory is giving way to what some philosophers of science call an "implicate or enfolded order"—a perspective which claims that only wholeness is real, that all "parts" of the universe, including the observer and that which is observed, are interpenetrating elements of one reality which is indivisible and nonanalyzable. This notion of an implicate order as "undivided wholeness in flowing movement," if internalized (made part of our personal way of seeing), represents a new reading of both text and context and has implications for all of life's projects.

Toward Rituals of Healing

What do all these scientific developments mean for the liturgist, whose specific purpose may be to create a ritual of healing?

It has often been argued that the Church *is* the context for liturgy. This is indeed a valid assumption. To take such a view seriously, however, in light of the complexities of "text," presents extraordinary challenges to the contemporary liturgist eager to make rites meaningful.

Ideally, of course, the hope would be that the ill person has so thoroughly internalized the context—that is, the total mission of the Church—that he or she receives the rite easily and with profound meaning. In this instance the ill person accepts joyfully a rite of healing with meaning in place. Text and context are as one. Meaning is assured.

But in our contemporary world both text and context have been enlarged and discovered to be multifarious and highly spirited, partly as a result of some of the scientific developments noted in this chapter. Indeed as our sample of the human sciences demonstrates, there are three massive principles constantly made manifest within empirical study: the person (text) is an assortment of intricate, complex, and ever-changing variables making up a *unique* system; the world as environment is an expansive, complex, and changing universe with commonality available but frequently conditioned by many factors; and the relationships between these two great galaxies is one of interdependence, interpenetration, and a flowing unity.

Before such an amazingly complex picture it would be tempting to settle for a simple and sovereign notion of context and worry little, if at all, about the text/context "fit." It might be argued, as has been done at times in the history of the Church, that Church as context is sufficient and that even a text outlandishly at variance with it can gain from the rite, for there is in each rite a sort of archetype of hope and promise that is bound "to get through" no matter the nature of the text.

Certainly the truth of this perspective is evident at times in both our personal histories and in the general history of the Church and its sacraments. Yet just as evident is the growing awareness that such a stance harbors dangers of alienation and an oversimplification of creation. Would it not be better to expand context to meet the growing reality of an evolving text so that text may discover context in a symbiotic fashion, where meaning, especially in the most cataclysmic of conditions, will be discovered?

References

Allport, Gordon W. *Pattern and Growth in Personality.* New York: Holt, Rinehart & Winston, 1961.

Bandler, Richard, and Grinder, John. *The Structure of Magic.* Palo Alto, Calif.: Science and Behavior Books, 1975. 2 vols.

Becker, Ernest. *The Denial of Death.* New York: The Free Press, 1973.

Chupunco, Anscar J. *Cultural Adaptation of the Liturgy.* New York: Paulist Press, 1982.

Colston, Lowell G., and Johnson, Paul E. *Personality and Christian Faith.* Nashville, Tenn.: Abingdon Press, 1972.

Cousins, Norman. *Anatomy of an Illness as Perceived by the Patient.* New York: Norton, 1979.

Friedman, Edwin H. *Generation to Generation: Family Process in Church and Synagogue.* New York: Guilford Press, 1985.

Gerkin, Charles V. *The Living Human Document.* Nashville, Tenn.: Abingdon Press, 1984.

Giorgi, Amendeo. *Psychology as a Human Science: A Phenomenologically Based Approach.* New York: Harper & Row, 1970.

Gleason, John J., Jr. *Consciousness and the Ultimate.* Nashville, Tenn.: Abingdon Press, 1981.

Gordon, David. *Therapeutic Metaphors.* Cupertino, Calif.: META Publications, 1978.

Irvin, Kevin W. *Liturgy, Prayer and Spirituality.* Ramsey, NJ: Paulist Press, 1980.

Israel, Martin. *Healing as Sacrament: The Sanctification of the World.* Cambridge, Mass.: Cowley Publications, 1984.

Kübler-Ross, Elisabeth. *On Death and Dying.* New York: Macmillan, 1969.

Kuhn, Thomas. *The Structure of Scientific Revolution.* Chicago: The University of Chicago Press, 1971.

Levine, Robert A. *Culture, Behavior, and Personality.* Chicago: Aldine Publishing, 1973.

Lonergan, Bernard J. F. *Method in Theology.* New York: Harper & Row, 1972.

McCormick, Richard A. *Health and Medicine in the Catholic Tradition.* New York: Crossroad, 1984.

May, Gerald G. *Care of Mind/Care of Spirit.* San Francisco: Harper & Row, 1982.

Reimer, Lawrence D., and Wagner, James T. *The Hospital Handbook: A Practical Guide to Hospital Visitation.* Wilton, Conn.: Morehouse and Barlow, 1984.

Smart, Ninian. *Worldviews: Crosscultural Explorations of Human Beliefs.* New York: Scribners, 1983.

Snyder, C. R., and Fromkin, Howard L. *Uniqueness: The Human Pursuit of Difference.* New York: Plenum Press, 1980.

Stafford, Harry C. *Culture and Cosmology: Essays on the Birth of World View.* Washington: University Press of America, 1981.

Strunk, Orlo, Jr. *Privacy: Experience, Understanding, Expression.* Washington: University Press of America, 1981.

Sugerman, A. Arthur, and Tarter, Ralph, eds. *Expanding Dimensions of Consciousness.* New York: Springer Publications, 1978.

Valle, Ronald S., and King, M. *Existential-Phenomenological Alternatives for Psychology.* New York: Oxford University Press, 1978.

van Kaam, Adrian. *Religion and Personality.* Denville, N.J.: Dimension Press, 1980.

Van Leeuwen, Mary Stewart. *The Person in Psychology.* Grand Rapids, Mich.: Eerdmans, 1985.

2. RITES OF HEALING:
A REFLECTION IN PASTORAL THEOLOGY

Jennifer Glen, C.C.V.I.

Yearning toward immortality, men and women have struggled from time immemorial against the limits imposed on human life by the inevitability of death. At the foot of that unyielding wall lie the shattered remnants of many a hope, many a dream, and many a vision upon which lives and relationships are built. Still we seem to be quite capable of veiling death behind a flurry of plans and activities designed as if tomorrow would stretch out forever. We must, if we are to live at all. Yet our imagined Eden conceals the serpent, forever lying in wait to strike down our dreams. Something as minor as a headache that intrudes on an afternoon's work or as overwhelming as advanced cancer of the lung that abruptly cuts off all future hopes arises to remind us that the body must in the end, in small ways and in great, betray the human spirit's hunger for life. We are determined dreamers though. We do not accept defeat lightly. Our history reveals our propensity to do endless, quixotic battle against all the experiences of limit which lie between us and the last great limit, death. We work on despite the headache, the chronic arthritis, the cancer. We look for causes and cures for every illness, as if we believed that one day we could cure even our very mortality. We offer one another comfort in our pain and we gather together in the presence of the mystery of sickness, of suffering, and of death to perform the rites which enable us to bear it. We may seem fools, perhaps, but courageous fools nonetheless. Even in the teeth of the apparent absurdity of life lived "unto death," the human spirit remains more often than is reasonable an indomitable spirit.

As Christians we trust we are not fools. We look to the Gospel of Jesus Christ, and what we read there is good news: life is lived through death to life, and healing is its pledge. There is ground in Jesus' living, dying, and rising for our efforts to cure the sick, for our ministry of mutual comfort in suffering, and for the rites with which we assemble to confront the realities of illness, pain, and death in our midst. In life and in Word, Christ entrusted to the Church the mandate to heal in his name wherever the Gospel is preached. Healing is not incidental but integral to the evangelical proclamation.

Before we can adequately project the future shape of the "rites of healing" through which the Church explicitly assembled as Church gives ritual expression to this mandate, the human sciences teach us that we must examine the foundations for a ritual ministry of healing in human experience as well as in a theological vision of the Church's mission to heal in Jesus' name. An informal survey of popular piety in those Churches which celebrate sacraments of sickness would no doubt reveal all too clearly how easily the interpretation and celebration of the rites can become distorted if we fail to appreciate them in their essential human and theological contexts. Detached from those contexts they can degenerate into magical prescriptions for cure, hastily sketched amulets against despair or simply empty, pious platitudes with which to cloak the anguish of sickness and of death.

Experience

A community's rites are rooted in its experience of life. They articulate, interpret, and thus transform that experience from chaos to meaning. Therefore our Church community's rites in sickness must arise from and address illness and healing as they are really experienced in our particular cultures if the rites are genuinely to affect the lives of community members. Orlo Strunk's challenge to pursue the interplay of text and context is critical to theological reflection as well as to the creation of liturgical rite.

Upon examination we find that the term sickness is itself already a cultural interpretation of a complex set of interrelated physical, psychological, and social experiences. What may be considered a natural—even inconsequential—part of ordinary life in one culture may be labeled and treated as sickness in another. The processes of aging are a classic instance. The word sickness identifies the ex-

periences in question as undesirable. Sickness cries out for cure.
Societies tend further to generate root metaphors through which
to make some sense of the sickness and to marshal the appropriate
response. The image itself thus becomes an integral part of the experiences of sickness and healing. For example if the cultural imagination interprets sickness as demonic possession, it thereby
determines how persons who fall sick will view themselves, how
they and others will behave, and what corrective response the society will make. Conditioned as we are by the medical sophistica-
tion of our own culture, we may find both image and response
amusingly naive, but we would be unwise to assume that our own
root metaphors of sickness and healing are unassailable.

At least until recently the cultural imagination of modern North
America was shaped in its vision of sickness and healing largely
by medical institutions, themselves produced by the cultural imagination first of industrial and then of technological society. In
those societal world views there is a tendency to perceive human
beings as isolated, even interchangeable functional mechanisms
within the complex systems of productivity. Sickness is imaged as
a condition of malfunction in which the mechanism breaks down,
either because of invasion from without by a hostile force, such
as a virus, or because of corrosion from within, such as cardiovas-
cular disease. Treatment is conceived under the corresponding imagery of combat, in which the foreign invader is repelled by more
powerful counteragents, or of repair, in which the damaged parts
are restored to working order or replaced by skilled technicians.
In an increasingly sophisticated and depersonalized system of functional specialization, these technicians may even operate in relative isolation from one another. The model is of a "high tech"
assembly line, where the microchips are made in one place, the main-
frame in another, and the software in yet another on the assumption that they will be compatible with one another when assembled
into a finished product. This represents the same kind of temptation to cold, distanced, mechanical ritual that Orlo Strunk cites at
the beginning of his reflections. We are all familiar with the tragic
ironies which sometimes result: the drowned child is resuscitated
by the paramedics on site, only to live on for years in an irrevers-
ible coma in the intensive care unit; the disease victim's medications cause secondary illnesses far more life-altering than the original
disease. Physiological life can be preserved at the expense of human
life. As the ethical questions loom larger in the popular imagina-

tion, it is easy to cast stones of blame at the medical technocrats. No doubt there is blame to be borne in that quarter. However, the fuller truth is that the society at large, which produces both doctor and patient, has for many years subscribed to the common root metaphors on which the technological model of sickness and healing is constructed.

Apart from medicine's perennial humanitarians, who have never succumbed to the technological world view in its more exaggerated forms, proponents of alternative images of humanity in sickness and in health have only recently begun to offer a serious challenge to the prevailing technological imagery. Although theorists and theories differ somewhat, these alternatives may be grouped under the general heading of holistic medicine. The holistic world view tends to perceive the human being not as a mechanism but as a delicately balanced ecology of body, spirit, and, in some schools of thought, cosmos. Strunk's description of the human personality as a "dynamic mutual interaction" of such "systems" as the "physical, social, economic, political, ecological, and spiritual" is an example of this approach. Sickness is interpreted as a sign that the balance has been disturbed, either within the personal ecology of the individual organism or in the interaction between organism and environment. For example some cases of cancer are seen to be the result of grief-related stress, which has left the person susceptible to the virus, either latent in the body or present in the environment. Treatment is directed not only toward the eradication of the physical pathology but also toward the restoration of equilibrium. Its root metaphor is neither combat nor repair, but reconciliation. The cancer patient, for instance, is helped to identify and resolve the experience of loss which gave rise to the original tension, as well as being treated for the resultant tumor. Specialists still exist in a holistic health care system, of course, but they work together toward a common goal, which may include not only the patient but the patient's family and other communitarian circles and even the physical environment. Thus the underlying anthropology is neither pluralistic nor individualistic, but relational. The human person is perceived and treated as the nexus of a complex network of intrapersonal, interpersonal, and sometimes transpersonal relationships. It is this network which constitutes the person's identity.

The holistic approach to the cause and cure of sickness, with its root metaphors of ecology and reconciliation and its foundational anthropological vision of humanity as relationship, has clearly begun to shape our cultural imagination with regard to illness and its treatment, though it has not yet entirely undermined the vast medical complexes built upon the older technological model. However, as it enters into our imagination and therefore our experience of sickness, it suggests itself as a potential heuristic tool with which to analyze and describe that experience in order to offer a theological interpretation and project a ministerial response founded in present cultural reality.

From this perspective we find that sickness and therefore healing can indeed be effectively described in multifaceted relational terms rather than in the purely physical. However, like all relational realities sickness is not a fixed entity, but a process which can best be described as it develops within and changes what we would ordinarily call a healthy life.

Although we tend to think that we live in an entirely objective world, the fact is that we actually conduct our lives in the world which we have constructed out of our own interpretations, learned and created, of our experience of objective reality. Orlo Strunk notes the current interest of the human sciences in this phenomenon of the idiosyncratic world view or metaphor, both interpretative filters for raw reality. The interpreted world is one which has meaning for us. That is, it is a network of relational interactions for which we have an adequate explanation, whether or not it is conceptualized, and within which we know how to behave. It is not fixed, of course. It expands as we integrate new experiences into the familiar patterns, particularly in our early years, but it strives to retain an essential continuity even as it develops. Unless we are confronted with a dramatic experience which calls it entirely into question, we do not often give it a great deal of conscious attention. We simply move comfortably within it from the familiar present into the predictable future.

Let us look at a concrete example from daily life prior to the onset of illness. One Thursday I am speeding along the local interstate, blissfully unaware of my speedometer, my mind on the meeting toward which I am heading, when I am interrupted by the wail of a siren and the flashing of lights behind me. Quite unreflectively I sort quickly through the known explanations for such phenomena: ambulance, fire truck, paramedics—but no, a check in the rearview mirror reveals the pursuing presence of a two-toned car whose driver is in uniform. Again unreflectively, I call into play the known relationship between speed limit signs, the reading on my speedometer, and the vehicle behind me, and I interpret correctly that I have incurred the just displeasure of a state trooper. Being a law-abiding sort, I behave according to convention and pull over. That situation has meaning for me. Suppose, however, that my reveries were interrupted not by siren and lights but by absolute silence and a greenish phosphorescent glow suddenly bathing the landscape. That situation has no meaning for me; I have no explanation for the interactions that caused the silence and the light, and I do not know how to behave. Indeed I am paralyzed into inaction until I decide whether, in my mind at least, I am driving into a summer storm or a "close encounter of the third kind."

Clearly expectation is essential to meaning. The expected future is the horizon within which we judge and interact with the present. On the highway the expected scenario between trooper and driver has potential variations, but the general pattern is predictable enough to enable me to cast the officer in the role of accuser and myself in that of offender and to determine my response in the time it takes the trooper to reach my car. If instead of ticketing me, the trooper were to pull out a sandwich and offer it to me, I would be apt to stammer, "But I don't understand!" and I would not know what to do. When the expected future is snatched away and replaced with some totally alien alternative, the present loses its meaning for me, until I can reconstruct a projected future within which to act. The projection need only be of the immediate future, and it may be very quickly made by the present-oriented spontaneous personality. But as long as I cannot conceive of what may happen, at least within foreseeable immediacy, I cannot direct my relational interactions, and therefore I cannot continue them.

The element of expectation might be described in the language of faith and hope. To follow the train of thought set out by William F. Lynch in his classic *Images of Hope*, hope is precisely the act of the imagination whereby we project the future as possible and as desirable. The content of the projection is the object of our hope. Hope's alternatives are dread, in which the projected future is undesirable, or despair, in which the future does not seem possible at all. The act of hope implies a certain faith, which religionists define as inclusive of trust and belief. On the highway I am driving toward my projected meeting, because I believe it will take place. The reason for my belief is that I trust the person who called it not to play practical jokes. Thus faith grounds the imaginative projections of hope. Religionists make a further distinction between the

primordial faith with which all human beings entrust themselves
to the mystery of life perceived as intrinsically valuable, and the
religious faith with which some human beings name and articulate
in conceptual belief statements the ultimate mystery perceived as
sustaining life.

Sickness always constitutes a disruption of expectation. Unless
we know without much doubt that it is imminent, perhaps because
we have been exposed to something or have begun to show the warning signs, we rarely grant it a place in our projections for the afternoon, or next week, or the next decade. Whether it befalls us
suddenly or develops slowly, whether it turns out to be minor or
chronic or terminal, it seems always to take us by surprise. We know
intellectually that we are ultimately finite, but we seem unprepared
for the limits beyond which our bodily being will not take us. Illness, therefore, deprives us of our projected future. In so doing,
particularly if it is serious, it threatens the destruction of faith and
hope. We have placed the most basic of unspoken trusts in our
bodily life, and it has betrayed us. Because of that betrayal we can
no longer place any real trust in the future. Hope requires that we
project that future as both possible and desirable. To the person
who is seriously ill, the future often seems to be neither. Time shrinks
to the eternal now, beyond which "be dragons"—in the words of
the ancient cartographers labeling the unknown edges of the world.
Beyond lies the ultimate betrayal which is death, now recognized
as certain even if not immediate. The vision of death lurking within
the experience of sickness seems to cut off the future absolutely,
at least from the experiential and imaginative viewpoint. With the
loss of the future goes the loss of meaning. That toward which life
was lived, however unreflectively, no longer gives purpose and direction to the many relationships which constitute our world. In the
face of the insuperable barrier of death, concealed behind the immediate limit of present sickness, life and its relationships threaten
to become absurd.

As Orlo Strunk insists, the actual extent of personal disruption
which occurs in a particular case will depend on all sorts of variables. The nature and severity of the illness, the cultural and personal history which have forged the sufferer's personal world, the
socioeconomic circumstances which condition it, and the religious
convictions which sustain it all have a part to play in shaping the
way sickness is experienced and the response it elicits in the concrete. Strunk prefaces his exposition of variables perceived as sig-

nificant from the point of view of the human sciences with a well-placed warning against squeezing individual experiences into the mold of generalizations at the expense of the sufferer. Nevertheless, let us attempt to identify at least some features of the common relational skeleton, so to speak, which constitutes the state of being sick in our society, in order to derive from it a corresponding vision of healing.

For purposes of analysis, let us use the example of a severe illness which requires hospitalization, on the theory that the extreme case brings to light the fundamental patterns latent in every illness. Return with me to my ill-fated attempt to reach that Thursday meeting. This time let us suppose that after accepting my speeding ticket, I take off again, more carefully, only to be halted by the dreadful pains which presage a massive coronary. In the space of a breath, the entire future as I had projected it in my imagination, from the meeting at the end of the interstate to all the other plans I had woven for a healthy life, is suddenly blotted out. Moreover, at least in the first stages of survival, I cannot even begin to construct another. Every end toward which my relational world was directed has vanished, leaving an unbearable void within which little seems to make sense or to matter. Since there is a state trooper not far behind me, I am lucky enough to get help almost immediately, and I am admitted to a coronary care unit. There, while the doctors are examining my heart for damage, let us examine the relational fabric of my life.

First, there is the sphere of the intrapersonal. Until this moment I had never paid much attention to my body, except to grumble at its tendency to metamorphosize anything that tasted good into fat. Most of the time I took for granted that it was there to do my bidding. Now, however, it looms at the forefront of my consciousness, as a stranger, a constraint upon my "self," and a threat to my survival as a person. It is no longer an integral part of my "self." Moreover I find that I am "falling apart" emotionally. I cry, I am angry, I feel guilty. In both the physical and the psychic sense I am no longer a whole person.

Moreover, as visitors are gradually allowed with greater frequency, my interpersonal relationships soon appear to have been similarly disrupted. I no longer seem able to communicate with my family and friends. We have ceased to share the everyday realm in which our personal worlds of meaning overlapped to give us a common ground on which to converse. I am confined to the nar-

row sick world, and they to the wider world of relative health. I
am concerned with the events that matter in my little world: what
tests they did this morning, how late my medications were, whether
the nice nursing assistant will be on duty tonight. They are concerned with the events of that other world to which I no longer
belong: the price of meat, Julie's boyfriend, that cute new fast food
commercial, the president's tax proposal. We have nothing to talk
about. We cannot enter into one another's frame of reference.

Besides I no longer play the old roles which defined my relationship to them: spouse sharing the responsibilities of the house-
hold, parent making authoritative decisions for the child, daughter
providing support for my aging mother. I am no longer useful to
them; I have no value. I take from others—their care, their concern, their encouragement—but I have nothing to give in return.
Mutuality has disappeared. Many of my decisions are made for me
by relatives, by doctors, by medical personnel. I am treated as a
child, or worse as an inanimate object incapable of assuming responsibility for her own person and her own life in even its simplest
expressions. In fact I am gradually relinquishing my customary social role of autonomous, responsible adult for what sociologists have
entitled the "sick role," the role of patient in the etymological sense
of one who passively suffers the action of others upon her. It is
characterized by regression, in which the patient slowly relinquishes
all power to the providers of care and begins to demand parental
attention from them. In the strict technological model of medical
care, it is the role upon which both the providers and the receivers
of care agree. In such a context the "natural narcissism" to which
Orlo Strunk alludes easily threatens to become radical self-
centeredness.

At the transpersonal level my relationship with any ultimate
ground for the life which has betrayed me so brutally is equally
threatened. The chaplain tries to tell me to put my faith not in life
but in God. I was a religious person, I believed in God. I prayed
and went to church, but now I am angry. The God I believed in
has let me down. Perhaps God is punishing me, though like Job
I cannot imagine what I have done to deserve this. Why me? Anyway God has grown silent, distant. I no longer know how to pray,
I cannot concentrate, I am too tired. And I cannot go to church
to find God there in company with those whose worship I used to
share.

Confronted with the inescapable prospect of my own death, if not now then surely one day, my world has shattered into pieces at my feet. I never expected this, and now I do not know what to do anymore. I suppose I should do something about it, about my person, about my loved ones, about my religion—but to tell you the truth, I do not know if I want to bother. What is the use? None of it makes any sense anymore anyway. The future is gone, meaning is gone. All the relationships which defined me—intrapersonal, interpersonal, and transpersonal—are in shambles. Heal that, if you will!

What must first be taken into account in any efforts to heal the human wounds opened by this experience of illness is that it is not the patient alone who is affected. Orlo Strunk highlights the significance of this point, as articulated in the organic metaphors of psychological systems theories for the psychotherapeutic community, and he points to its implications for all forms of nonmedical care of the sick. The point will be further developed later by Mary Frances Duffy in the essay accompanying her rite for the families of the ill. When sickness becomes public in our midst, we are all confronted with our common mortality made manifest in the person of the sick one. The future seems suddenly less reliable for each of us. We whisper secretly: "John? He's two years younger than I am. What if it were me?" The future is particularly altered for those who belong to the sick person's immediate circle of family and friends. In different ways and to different degrees their relational worlds too are fragmented. The spouse faces the prospect of life with a dependent partner or with none. The parent sees vanishing all the dreams invested in the child. The child loses the reliable source of nurture and authority, at least for as long as the parent is ill and perhaps beyond, knowing now that the parent is a fragile being who will eventually die. Intimate friends, whose significance in a society comprised of growing numbers of single adults still goes largely unrecognized in medical, social, and pastoral care programs, face the particular loneliness of those who have no established family circle. Other friends, coworkers, employers must reorganize their lives temporarily or permanently around the lacuna left by the person who has fallen ill. The local bank, the volunteer organization, the political party—every social unit in which the person participated is affected in ever-widening circles. The sick person may in fact be described not as the sole victim but as the focal center of the social experience to which we give the name of sickness.

What then is healing? According to the nature of sickness as interpreted by the technological models as we have seen, it is primarily a matter of repairing the mechanism, at least insofar as that is possible. The larger rents in the relational fabric of human life can then be mended later under some other rubric and by other hands. There is a certain truth to this perspective. Physiological pathology lies at the heart of the larger experience to which we give the name of sickness. The removal of that pathology is therefore an important step in the healing process. However, it is not always possible. One of the serious limitations of this model as a potential heuristic foundation for the description of the Church's ministry of healing is that it has little but the possible alleviation of pain to offer to the chronically and terminally ill. In consequence, as the seminal work of Elisabeth Kübler-Ross revealed some time ago, the technological establishment tends to neglect these living symbols of its limits. A second limitation, equally serious in the light of the social nature of sickness, is that the technological model does not address the needs of family and friends who are co-sufferers with the sick. The scope of its definition of healing, therefore, seems rather narrow for our purposes as Church. Let us call its goal "cure" and view it as integral to but not exhaustive of "healing."

A holistic approach offers a different perspective on healing. If the experience of sickness is interpreted as the disintegration of our relational world in confrontation with our mortality, then healing must be interpreted as the reintegration of that world within some bearable perspective on the future. A holistic model of healing based on the perspective of this chapter would in fact include not a mere restitution but a transformation of the sufferers' world within a framework of meaning enlarged to embrace the reality of death. Such a model seems to allow scope for healing to take place even in the absence of cure. Moreover it concerns itself not only with the sick but also with their co-sufferers, to whom both Orlo Strunk and Mary Frances Duffy draw attention in their respective chapters. The holistic model, therefore, seems to be more congenial than does the technological model to serve as an approach which might animate the healing ministry of the Church. However, it must be tested against a theological interpretation of sickness and healing rooted in the mission of Jesus Christ.

Theology

The cultural interpretations through which we experience and respond to sickness serve as only one foundation for our ecclesial ministry of healing. As the previous paragraphs suggest, these interpretations must be evaluated in the light of a theological vision of healing rooted in the healing ministry of Jesus Christ. However, it is not enough simply to read in the Gospel accounts that Jesus cured the sick and commissioned the disciples to do the same in his name. From a fundamentalist point of view, the logical conclusion is that the Church must continue simply to offer physical cure following the technological model and perhaps by nonmedical means. Jesus clearly did not despise the desire of the sick to be made well, and neither may we, but the scope of his healing and ours is broader than cure. Otherwise, his ministry and ours are doomed to the same defeat as every other human enterprise against the iron wall of death, which undoes every cure in the end. However, if we read the Gospel narratives of healing by the theological light in which they appear to have been written, we discover that they serve as yet one more manifestation of the all-encompassing purpose to which the entire being and life of Jesus Christ was and is still dedicated. It is in the more comprehensive context of the eschatological mission of Christ that the theology of sickness and healing must be understood.

Biblical and postbiblical traditions provide us with a number of images and concepts through which to summarize the goal of Jesus' mission: salvation, redemption, atonement, heaven, and reconciliation are but a few. However, one of the most pervasive and powerful of the Gospel images, and one that seems to have been claimed by Jesus as central, is "the reign of God."

This "reign of God" is not a reality which can be captured in concept. Old and New Testament texts offer us tantalizing hints and glimpses instead. "The reign of God is like . . .": the garden of lost innocence which we imagine as our beginning and yearn for as our end (Gen 1-2); the mountain home from which God banishes all harm and hurt and to which God invites the nations for a great feast (Isa 11:9; 25:1-10); the "peaceable kingdom" where lion and lamb lie down together with a little child to lead them (Isa 11:6-8); the banquet table at which Jesus presides and at which the poor and outcast sit as honored guests (see all Gospels); the mustard bush, growing everywhere unnoticed under our feet (see Matt 13:31-32); the pearl worth the sale of a lifetime's lesser treasures (see Matt 13:44-46); the great city, the new Jerusalem, where God and humanity dwell together in the light that streams from the throne where the slain lamb reigns in glory (Rev 21). These and a myriad of other images tease our vision, tug at our dreams, and haunt our hearts with invitation. From the Gospel texts we have some glimmer of the life to which they summon us. We have heard its ethic proclaimed in the Sermon on the Mount and summarized in the two great commandments. We have seen its promise mirrored in lepers healed and in lame beggars leaping, in blind eyes opened and in mute tongues singing praises. We have heard tales even of the dead being raised to life. We have met the reign of God fully realized in the communion of godhead and humanity revealed in the Word made flesh and raised beyond death to glory through the Cross. Jesus proclaimed the reign of God in word, in deed, and ultimately in the very fabric of his being and life. Indeed it is his own life and the lives of the many communities of his disciples that Christ offers as the strongest guarantor that the reign of God is a possible, even a desirable, future for humanity, because its signs are already appearing in our midst.

The reign of God cannot be captured in concept, because it is a multifaceted image that defies reduction. However, we can sketch its outlines conceptually by saying that it is a present glimpse and a future promise of all things brought to wholeness in Jesus Christ, from the divided self symbolized in the Gerasene demoniac inhabited by "Legion" (Mark 5:1-10) to the divided cosmos imaged as creation groaning to be set free (Rom 8:22). Jesus revealed the "inbreaking" of the reign of God in human history when he restored the individuals rent apart by the demons of madness, disease, guilt, and whatever other dark forces lurk in the depths of the human heart waiting to tear us asunder. He revealed it when he restored the families and communities torn apart by the death of a daughter, a son, a brother, or by the exclusion of a leper, an adulteress, a taxgatherer. Paul and John promised it when they dreamed of a new humanity growing into the oneness of the Body of Christ, of all the powers of the cosmos being brought under the one power of Jesus Christ, and of all reality being made one in Christ and through Christ taken at last into that communion where God will be all in all. The reign of God, then, is the final realization of our ever incipient human wholeness—personal, social, cosmic—the communion of all human beings with each other and with God in Jesus Christ.

Within the framework of this strong biblical image of the goal of Jesus' mission, we can understand why healing emerges as one of the principal activities of that mission. As we have already seen, sickness is an experience of fragmentation. The relationships which describe person, community, society, cosmos, and the ultimate mystery of transcendence within which they reside are sundered by the confrontation with death in the person of the sick one. Because this fragmentation stands in direct opposition to the goal of Jesus' mission rendered in obedience to the will of God, it may be described as a manifestation of the reign of evil, that is, the antithesis of the reign of God. This is not to say, as do some popular theologies of sickness, ancient and modern, that sickness is punishment for personal sin. It is rather one of many manifestations of the radical disorder of creation to which we give the name original sin. Healing is an integral part of the mission of Jesus to transform every manifestation of fragmentation into wholeness. Healing itself, then, is far more than cure, though it may include cure. In the Gospel miracle narratives cure is the sign and pledge of the fullness of healing in which is realized and revealed the reign of God irrupting into human history. That healing is the reconciliation of every relationship disrupted by sickness. However, where the words cure and reconciliation may imply a return to a former state of wholeness, healing in the fullest Gospel sense implies instead a transformation of perspective within which human life and relationships take on a new meaning unbounded by death. In the pasch of Jesus Christ, every human future opens out definitively into the reign of God. Within that ultimate horizon faith and hope transcend absurdity and give reason to pursue the growth toward communion in love which is the moral imperative of every Christian life. Healing in this context, then, consists ultimately in the offer and acceptance of this eschatological perspective as the ground upon which present relationships can be reconstructed toward wholeness at every level in the trust and hope that they are the radical presence of the future coming into being in our midst. The inner core of healing is conversion.

Ministry

Of course healing does not begin with the ultimate but with the immediate. According to the Gospel accounts Jesus himself did not begin with mere word of promise but with cure and reconciliation: the demoniac exorcized and restored to "himself" (see Mark 20); the little girl raised and reunited with her parents (see Mark 5:35-43); the leper cleansed and readmitted to his community (see Mark 1:40-44). Only on the ground of such living and tangible signs of human brokenness made whole did he lay claim to his listeners' trust and hope in the coming of the reign of God, with his own life and death and resurrection as its strongest pledge. As heir to the mandate to heal in his name, the Church is equally responsible for cure and for reconciliation within the context of its mission to proclaim the good news of salvation to "those who sit in darkness and in the shadow of death" (Luke 1:79).

As Church, therefore, we must be prepared to embrace a vision of our healing ministry more comprehensive than we sometimes credit. It is a ministry which has at least three components: societal, medical, and pastoral. Those who pursue the systemic social causes and cures of illness, those who search out and treat its medical dimensions, and those who attempt to remedy the psychological, social, and spiritual divisions it causes are all participants in the one work of making whole the human beings and communities torn asunder by illness. This is not the place to argue the theological significance of such work when it is not done expressly in the name of Jesus Christ, though we might recall that Jesus himself is reported to have rebuked jealous disciples for assuming that non-member exorcist-healers could not do the work of the reign of God (see Luke 9:49-50). We must further beware of the temptation to fall into the assumptions of the technological model of medical care, which permits society to delegate each of these works to a functional specialist and thereby to discharge its corporate responsibility. The work of healing, in the comprehensive Christian sense, falls not only to professional medical, social, and pastoral personnel but to all of us who are neighbor to the sick and their co-suffering families and friends. To visit the sick, to care for children so a spouse can spend time with an ill spouse, to provide meals for the disrupted family, and to pray with the sufferers are only some of the forms this informal neighborly pastoral ministry of healing can take.

Not least does the work of healing, in the fullest Christian sense, fall to the sufferers themselves. In this regard the Christian understanding of the baptismal commitment to the Church's mission in every circumstance of life stands in stark contrast to the technological culture's perception of the sick person as "patient" in the etymological sense. In technological centers of medical care, the family assumes a corresponding role of helpless appendage to the treatment provided by the professionals. The culture invites the sick and their co-sufferers to relinquish responsibility for others; the Church challenges them to assume it. The natural preoccupation with self-preservation, to which Orlo Strunk adverts, is challenged by an ethic of responsibility for neighbor. To extend an idea developed by David Power, the sick person and all those whose worlds are tangibly disrupted by that person's sickness are themselves summoned to serve as sacrament. In them the human confrontation with death is made public in the midst of the community. In them the human choices of despair and hope are made clear. Their struggle to find grounds to live in concert with the Gospel commandment of selfless love within the Christian eschatological vision is our common struggle in the face of our universal mortality. Their conversion from question to conviction, from a world shattered by death to a world made whole again in the very teeth of death, is the sacramental manifestation of the Pasch of Christ lived out at the heart of human history. Thus in their own lives, perhaps enabled by all who have ministered to them, they themselves stand witness before the rest of the Church, and indeed before all of fragile humanity to whom the Church is in mission, to the eschatological healing toward which all works of cure and reconciliation are directed.

We must appreciate this full scope of the Church's ministry in sickness, lest we distort the ritual expression of that ministry by inflating or misplacing it. The rites of healing are the Church's solemn symbolic proclamation of the reign of God as the ultimate framework of meaning within which to rebuild the relational world shattered by the confrontation with death. As Strunk recognizes, they serve to communicate meaning. They neither preempt nor substitute for the more immediate work of cure and reconciliation as the tangible signs which clothe with credible flesh the promise of hope offered in the name of a loving God. To paraphrase the familiar words of John's first letter (1 John 4:20), if sufferers cannot trust the concrete healing care of the Christian community they can see, how can they be asked to trust the ultimate healing care of the community's Lord, whom they cannot see? However, just as the human experiences of cure and reconciliation at one another's hands makes credible the promise that heals, so also the acceptance of that promise deepens the experiences of cure and reconciliation. It is not unlikely for the sick to recover unexpectedly after participating in the rites of the Church. Given the contemporary understanding of the relationship between psyche and soma, we need not resort to magic or even to miracle to explain that when the ills of the spirit—such as anxiety and despair—are healed through a renewal of faith and of hope, the ills of the body may sometimes disappear. However, whether or not bodily recovery occurs, that same renewal of faith and of hope, and therefore of a sense of value and purpose to life beyond the immediacy of illness, constitutes the context for full reconciliation with one's self, with one's loved ones, with one's various communities, and with one's environment, all within the sphere of reconciliation with the God of the future present in Jesus Christ. Thus the works of cure and reconciliation and the ritual revelation of their eschatological significance do not fall into the technological categories of functional specialties only tangentially related. On the contrary, although they are spread among a variety of people who work properly within their own spheres of competency, they are nevertheless inseparably joined under the one mandate of the Church to heal in Jesus' name.

In order to pursue further the proper role and possible forms of ritual within this multifaceted ministry of healing, we must examine certain key insights into the nature and function of rite itself, insofar as they contain critical implications for the future shape of the Church's rites of healing. Space will permit us only the briefest of summaries. Rite is the corporate symbolic action through which the community imposes the order of interpretation on the chaos of its experience. Our rituals do not add some superfluous explanation to what we have experienced after the fact. Rather, they provide direction for the living interaction of understanding and experience as our lives unfold. We live in the world of meaning established by our rites. For example, at least in time gone by and in some social circles, it was the rites of graduation rather than the four years of study which provided the twenty-two-year-old with the identity of adult now capable of and responsible for adult roles in society. Any former student knows that it takes some time after graduation to grow into that identity in all its implications. Consistent with the holistic description of identity as a network of relationships, rite is the symbolic articulation of just such networks. In the highly concentrated symbolic language of its rituals, the community both expresses the relational patterns which currently define it and sets out the relational patterns toward which it aspires as its ideal. Prescinding from the anthropological controversy over the relationship between story and rite, the symbolic ritual complex of word and action permits the community to own both present reality and future hope and to negotiate the dangerous passage between the two. The entire community, as well as its individual members, lives in the relational world established by its rites. When change threatens community stability, the rites enable community members to reaffirm the community's enduring identity in terms of the constant goal toward which they live and by which they define themselves. Ritual is therefore a concrete communal act of hope and of faith, through which the community imagines the future as both possible and desirable. It thus makes the present bearable in light of the future into which it is expected to open out, however slowly and painfully. Christian ritual in time of suffering is the Church's symbolic proclamation of the Christian eschatological vision offered for the Church's appropriation. Through that appropriation the community of sufferers is ultimately healed. The healing cannot be forced, however. The repetitive symbolic language of the rite has enormous power gradually to form and thus ultimately to transform our worlds of meaning. However, that transformation is an act of grace, to which we can open ourselves through the credible mutual ministries of cure and reconciliation but which we can never engineer through our manipulation of the rites, however learned and clever we may think ourselves to be.

Experience, theology, and the intrinsic nature and goal of the Church's ritual ministry of healing all serve to generate creative insights into the future shape of that ministry. Let us sketch those insights here, using examples from present rites as illustrations and leaving to others the task of putting new ritual flesh on these bare bones.

Toward Rituals of Healing

From our analysis of experience, we first recall that sickness and therefore healing are social rather than a merely physical processes. Our exploration of the theology of healing in Jesus' name has further emphasized the fact that the ultimate goal of Christian healing is essentially a complex relational rather than mere physical wholeness. Given in addition the relational nature of ritual per se, we must conclude that the Church's rites of healing are intrinsically communal actions in which both the community and its sufferers interact in a mutual invitation to accept the transformation of their worlds of meaning in light of the eschatological future present in Jesus Christ. As a symbolic event which reveals the deepest meaning of the ministries of cure and reconciliation already taking place among those engaged in this particular sickness, the ritual assembly ought ideally to include significant representatives of all the participants in this shared experience, if not all the participants themselves. It is these people who constitute most concretely the human social body shattered and in need of transformation toward eschatological reconciliation, a point taken up in the ritual essays of both Mary Frances Duffy and Gerald Calhoun. The rites should presuppose their participative presence as the norm, though of course a certain amount of pastoral creativity would be necessary actually to bring them together out of the religious diversity of a pluralistic society. This provision reflects the long wisdom of the Orthodox Churches, where the communal nature of the rite of holy unction has been firmly respected. It runs counter to the pastoral traditions of those Churches which have tended to reduce the ritual assembly to a quasi-private encounter between minister and patient, an option still implicitly available in the renewed Roman Catholic (*Pastoral Care of the Sick*, 1983) and Lutheran rites (*Occasional Services*, 1982 companion to *The Lutheran Book of Worship*).

Moreover, the rites must not only gather but also in some sense address all the members of this significative assembly. The sick person is not alone in the experience of sickness. The sick person alone is not the only one to be addressed by the symbolic healing word. This point is the focus of Duffy's rite for the families of the sick and is of concern to Calhoun. It is acknowledged implicitly in the Lutheran "Service of the Word for Healing" (*Occasional Rites*), which is more expansive in its intercessory prayer for all sufferers in general and for the families and medical attendants of the sick than are, for example, the Roman Catholic rites. However, the Lutheran texts seem to envision the family and medical staff most explicitly in their function as ministers to the sick. Whatever the strengths and limitations of specific rites, Christian ministry to those affected by sickness differs radically in all its forms from the technological model of medical care which concerns itself solely with the sick person as an isolated individual.

However, rite requires focus, lest it becomes so diffuse as to dissipate its power to address the issue of ultimate meaning in the midst of very particular human experiences. What is required, then, is that full play be given to the complex ambiguity of symbolic ritual language, which permits the unifying focus to become a condensed expression of the whole. Thus the sick person and perhaps the sick person's immediate circle of co-sufferers become the prism through which the rites speak inclusively to the experience of the entire community in its confrontation with mortality. The Roman Catholic rite of Communion for the sick (*Pastoral Care of the Sick*) is an interesting example. The assembly has gathered explicitly for the Communion of a particular sick person. Yet all of the rubrics indicate that the texts are directed to "the sick person and all present." Therefore every facet of healing invoked upon the sick person, from the peace of the initial greeting to the strength of the final blessing, may appear to be most appropriate to the sick person alone but is actually tacitly invoked upon the entire assembly. However, Duffy notes the limitation of this style of indirect ministry to the co-sufferers of the sick.

The communal nature of the rites of healing holds yet another implication for their celebration. Not only are they addressed to the entire body assembled to be healed, they are addressed by the members of the body speaking the transforming promise of Jesus Christ to one another out of their common mandate as Church to heal in his name. The rites summon the Church to mutual responsibility; therefore they must express that summons by engaging assembly members in a diversity of ministries ritually expressive of the eschatological significance of the ministries of cure and reconciliation they offer one another outside the ritual setting. This includes not only the commonly accepted liturgical ministries of leadership in prayer and song, proclamation of the Word, and distribution of the Eucharist, to which ancient Church writers attached the image of medicine for eternal life. It also implies the need to provide an appropriate ritual role for the sick and their co-sufferers as responsible participants in the Church's mission. Here the revised worship books of the Episcopalian (*Book of Common Prayer*, 1979), Lutheran, and Roman Catholic Churches provide instructive examples of the traditional ritual neglect of the ministry of the sick to the community. Although the general introduction to *Pastoral Care of the Sick* develops the notion of the paschal sacramentality of the sick, the rites themselves, like those of the Lutheran and Episcopalian rituals, cast the sick person in the role of passive recipient of the ministries of others.

The final implication of the communal nature of the rites of healing draws our attention to the community's transcendent referent. We must remember that the Church's rites engage us not only in intrapersonal and interpersonal interactions toward full reconciliation but also in a transpersonal relationship. They are at root communal acts of worship addressed to the God revealed to us in history as the source of all healing. This suggests that, like all the liturgical acts of the Church, they must be patterned on the paradigmatic act of worship, which is Eucharist. It is only in the context of memorial and thanksgiving that the Christian community makes petition to the God remembered and acknowledged as good. This communal affirmation of faith in the sometimes incomprehensible fidelity of God as Savior throughout history is particularly important in time of sickness, where precisely that faith has been called into question. Both the Orthodox and the Lutheran rites for the sick, with their strong doxological component, serve as examples of rituals which intend to call the Church to worship in the midst of suffering.

We have already noted that sickness, healing, and ritual are not discrete relational interactions but relational processes. They are not single events but relationships which develop over time. Therefore it seems apparent that the Church's rites of healing must be so structured as to accompany and direct movement along the relational continuum from sickness to healing. Both Orlo Strunk and Mary Frances Duffy suggest the potential value and the limitation of Elisabeth Kübler-Ross' stage theory for this correlation of rite and experiential progression. Gerald Calhoun identifies shifts in emphasis which might characterize the rite of anointing the sick at different moments in the unfolding of sickness. However, what might appear a simple observation concerning the necessity of relating rite to process conceals several implications which place heavy demands upon those who develop actual rituals. First, the rites must articulate honestly the tension between suffering and hope. The contemporary literature of grief has made us well aware that our first response to sickness and suffering is usually denial. We can ask our rituals to collude in that denial by offering empty assurances that "all will be well and all manner of things will be well" in some roseate future which bears no living relationship to our present pain. However, there can be no genuine movement toward healing that does not begin with a truthful acknowledgement of the brokenness that needs to be made whole. Therefore we ought rightly to ask our rituals to permit us to see what we dare not see and to say what we dare not say. The lectionary in *Pastoral Care of the Sick* (PCS 297–298) offers a prime example. Three of its Old Testament selections are taken from the dreadful laments of the Book of Job (Job 3:3, 11-17, 20-23; 7:1-4, 6-11; 7:12-21). They are simply howls of angry pain, without resolution. They seem at first glance to offer no comfort. Yet in fact they offer to the sick and their co-sufferers the inexpressible comfort of giving voice with impunity to the worst of their feelings in the presence of the community and of God. Once owned in ritual, the anguish has permission to be owned in life. Once the suffering is owned, the sufferer is freed to accept healing.

In addition to confronting suffering truthfully, the rites must walk the delicate line between universality and particularity. Ultimately the shattering and reconstituting of all human worlds before the truth of our death is the paschal story of every person. However, every person's progress from sickness to healing differs, even within the one community assembled around the one experience of sickness. The rituals must engage the personal experience of each one in our common paschal mystery, but they cannot realistically follow the individual twists and turns of every person's path. In his closing remarks Strunk seems to suggest the near impossibility of the task. Yet effective symbolic language has the capacity to catch the particular up in the universal. The lectionary might once again serve as a case in point. While many of the biblical narratives chosen by the rituals of the various Churches for use with the sick tell the story of the particular individuals now long dead, they continue to engage the experience of contemporary sufferers. The laments from Job found in the Roman Catholic lectionary, for example, are attributed by the book's final editor to a folktale figure, but they still bespeak powerfully the torment of every human spirit afflicted with the universal mystery of loss. Some of the rituals encourage the use of the sufferers' names as a way of personalizing the universal texts of collects and blessings. However, Calhoun may have identified the real key to personalization in his articulation of the pastoral relationship itself as the most powerful mediator of appropriate personal meaning, whatever the structure and content of its ritual expression. His reflection reminds us that the true rite is the rite celebrated in the concrete human context of a particular assembly sharing a particular experience, rather than the rite as recorded in the pages of a ritual book.

Finally, with reference to the rites as process, it seems almost superfluous to say that the Church's ritual repertoire must include a variety of rites which constitute a coherent as well as flexible progression through various stages of the passage from sickness to healing, even where no physical change takes place. One example is the comprehensive set of rites offered for all stages of illness— from the minimal through the terminal—in *Pastoral Care of the Sick*. Some of these rites should be capable of frequent repetition as needed, such as the rite of Communion. Others should be directed toward critical moments in the progression, such as the Roman rite of anointing the sick, which may be repeated over the course of an illness but not with the frequency of Communion. It is important to recognize more explicitly than we sometimes do that despite the narrowed vision of tradition suggested by a reading of medieval rituals out of context, even the most sacramental of Churches have rarely, if ever, viewed the anointing of the sick as the sum total of the Church's ritual intervention in sickness.

In our reflections thus far we have considered both the structures and the content of rites of healing from the point of view of the relational and processive nature of sickness, healing, and rite. A more particular focus on the eschatological goal of the Church's ritual ministry to those affected by sickness draws us into a further concern for content. In the postconciliar retrieval of a sacramental ministry to the sick, as opposed to the narrower medieval and post-medieval tradition of a sacramental ministry largely directed toward the dying, and in the development of more charismatic forms of ritual ministry to the sick, the Churches tended at first to lean heavily on biblical passages and prayers which promised physical cure, perhaps in an understandable reaction against the long popular Roman emphasis on "curing" the soul through forgiveness while the body lay dying. While cure is certainly important, especially to the sick and their immediate circle, it is never more than a partial goal, eventually to be undone by death in one form or another. As we have seen, it is only one aspect of the healing sought by the Church in its ritual ministry. Even where cure is impossible, as it often is in cases of chronic or terminal illness, healing is still requested and received. Therefore the texts and actions of the rites must be carefully selected to put cure in its proper perspective as one—albeit much-desired—pledge of the more comprehensive reality of eschatological healing. They must not make false or exaggerated promises of cure, against which God will be tried and found wanting by sufferers who find no medical relief. Rather, they must challenge participants to faith and to hope without denying the truth of suffering and of the desire to get well. Some of the collects of the Episcopalian, Lutheran, and Roman Catholic rites for the sick serve as examples of texts which must be selected with care, lest they be heard as ineffective prayers to an incompetent God for impossible cures, which do not in fact materialize.

Not only the nature of sickness and of Christian healing but also the nature of ritual itself dictates some aspects of the shape of the Church's ritual ministry to the sick. To recall an earlier paragraph, the language of ritual is symbolic: symbolic words, symbolic actions, symbolic postures, symbolic spaces, symbolic objects, symbolic clothing, and so on. It is of the nature of symbol to be allusive rather than explicit, affective rather than conceptual, ambiguous rather than univocal. One of the dangers of attempting to refashion our rites for the sick is that we will reduce them to unimaginative doctrinal or moral exhortations rather than permitting them to be richly evocative glimpses into the reign of God as the hope of the sufferer. Perhaps it is wiser to read the story of the stilling of the storm (Matt 8:23-27) than to read the tale of the leper's cleansing (Matt 8:2-4); perhaps it is enough to offer the Blood of Christ rather than to expound on the presence of the crucified and risen healer; perhaps it is more telling to impose hands in silence than to drown the action's intrinsic power in a river of explanation. In time of pain, we do not need lengthy explanations as much as we need stories; we do not need doctrinal expositions as much as we need the terse and imaginative "great words," as Karl Rahner once called them, which capture the whole truth of years of experience in the space of one or two syllables; we do not need moral exhortations as much as we need the simple reassurance of touch, of bread broken and shared, of oil poured out soothingly with a lavish hand.

As these examples indicate, symbolic ritual language employs not one idiom but many. It speaks not only to the disembodied intellect but to the enfleshed spirit. It engages every dimension of our human being: sight, hearing, smell, touch, speech, and song. It brings us to wholeness by engaging the whole person, as well as the whole community of persons, in a single unifying act of meaning. Even imaginative words are not enough, especially in times of anguish when words seem sometimes hollow. If the sick person finds him or herself alienated from personal bodily reality, perhaps the rite should demand that the sick person participate precisely as an integrated bodily person through such postures and gestures as physical circumstances permit. If the family is turned in upon itself in its suffering, perhaps the rite should invite family members to offer the Communion cup to friends and neighbors. If friends have isolated the sick person by showing revulsion for the betraying body, perhaps the rite should challenge them to lay hands upon their ailing friend and thus commit themselves to action to the reconciliation into which they hope to grow. The rites should not neglect any of their potential idioms: friends gathered in the lonely homes of the sick; songs sung against the silence of those whom despair has rendered mute; colored vestments bringing life to the sterile whites of the sick world; good-tasting bread and wine enjoyed amid the chemical tastes of medicines; incense enriching the odorous world of sicknesses and disinfectants; paschal candles burning beneath the artificial glare of the institution's flourescent lights. The richly symbolic rite of holy unction, as celebrated in the Orthodox Churches, is a wonderful example of a multilingual act of prayer, incorporating such dimensions as assembly, chant, gesture, wheat, wine, oil, incense, and vesture (see, for example, the *Service Book of the Holy Orthodox-Catholic Apostolic Church*, 1975, 332–359, 607–609).

As symbolic actions the rites of healing cannot, any more than any other ritual, be created anew of whole cloth. Genuine symbols are given rather than fabricated. They come to us out of the depths of our human psychic, social, and cosmic experience. For example we learn from infancy that food is the tangible expression of love from the one on whom we depend for the life of our bodily and psychosocial self. Food stills our deep-seated fear of isolation and annihilation. What stronger symbolic response could a community gathered in the name of the Lord make to the experience of sickness than to offer the ritual food of the Eucharist shared at the common table of the reign of God? Symbols have their origin in experience, but they gather depth and nuance of meaning as they interact with the cumulative experience of the community over time. Unless they die before they disappear from the community's tradition, they reach us profoundly enhanced by the wisdom of generation upon generation of our forebears who have grappled, as we grapple now, with the profound mysteries of life and death. Moreover, the great symbols accompany us from childhood into old age, acquiring personal meaning for us as they are woven into the cumulative texture of our own lives through moments of sorrow and joy, confusion and insight. For example, if we have prayed the Lord's Prayer in solitude and in community, day in and day out, from a parent's knee into adulthood, we may find extraordinary meaning in repeating the familiar words in the midst of the sickness which has robbed life of every other familiar landmark. The phrases, "Thy kingdom come; thy will be done . . . lead us not into temptation, but deliver us from evil," pierce our chaos with new light; the experience of chaos reveals new depths in the age-old phrases. The revised rites of the Episcopalian, Lutheran, and Catholic Churches all include this familiar prayer from our everyday lives, which is likely to offer us greater comfort and challenge than will any of the newer texts addressed to such contemporary circumstances as preparation for surgery (see *Pastoral Care of the Sick,* 125E) or making decisions concerning life-support systems (see "Service of the Word for Healing," 17g). If we are caught up in suffering, either physical or emotional, we may not even be able to take in the new word. All we can cling to is the old. Moreover we need ritual words and actions and objects which enable us to bridge the gap between the unfamiliar experience of sickness and the familiar world from which it has alienated us. We need rites to make new sense out of our everyday lives, both past and present, so we can indeed live those lives within the eschatological world of meaning into which the rites call us. This means that the rites must somehow open up the deep meaning of the ordinary through the ritual inclusion of symbolic persons, words, actions, objects, drawn from our ordinary world. It is of the very nature of ritual to take up these significant elements of the everyday, condense and intensify them, and thus reveal their depths. For example in the sick world with its medications and medicinal rubs, it is valuable to call upon the ancient imagery of the Eucharist as the medicine of eschatological healing, or of oil as the soothing, strengthening, healing unguent for the aching, weakened person who is sick.

This is not to say that there is no place for the new symbolic word, the new gesture, or the new object in our rites for the sick. Ritual studies suggest that familiarity is indeed a key to ritual prayer. Rites cannot become prayer until they are well polished by use. Moreover, they cannot shape our Christian vision in prayer unless they are repeated again and again. That is the nature of rite. However, ritual studies also indicate that rite incorporates into the familiar repeated patterns moments of novelty which can startle us into new insight at significant moments. The new word spoken in the midst of sickness to a community formed by the accustomed patterns of prayer may indeed be the catalyst for transformation. The key to be sought is an appropriate balance between the familiar and the new in the shaping of the rites. For example the general structure of the Roman rite of viaticum, Communion for the dying, is the same as that of every Communion rite, with one telling exception. After the well-known prayers have been said and Communion given to the dying person, the minister adds: "May the Lord Jesus Christ protect you and lead you to eternal life" (PCS 207). Thus the structure and content of the rite both express the continuity of this act of Communion with every other act of Communion the person has made and at the same time draws attention to the new meaning of Communion received in immediate preparation for the final pasch.

These sketchy projections of directions for ritual development based on a reflection on the experience and theology of sickness and healing as well as upon the intrinsic nature and goal of the Church's ritual ministry to the sick—regardless of the structure and content of its particular rites—have perhaps raised as many questions as they have answered for those who would shape the future of the rites. One critical question which has not been and cannot be addressed within the scope of this chapter is the distinction to be made between rites of healing specifically intended for those affected by physical sickness and more generic rites of healing intended for those affected by other forms of personal disruption. Healing is a popular word in contemporary culture and therefore in our contemporary Churches. It is used not only to describe the treatment of sickness, but to describe the resolution of almost every form of relational conflict imaginable. Indeed with some justification from tradition, it tends to be used in ecclesial circles as the universal metaphor for every exercise of the Church's mission of redemptive reconciliation. As we have seen, the metaphor is not inapt. The dissolution of one's relational world of meaning is not unique to sickness. Therefore healing, in the ultimate sense of conversion to a Christian eschatological vision within which one's world can be reconstituted, is indeed an image interchangeable with reconciliation in its fullest sense. Are the Church's specifically designated rites of healing, then, to be rites of reconciliation equally appropriate for those whose lives have been disrupted by bodily illness and those whose lives have been disrupted by some other form of suffering?

The borderline case seems to be the person who suffers from what North American culture currently calls mental or emotional illness. While certain dissenters from the medical establishment argue that the relational patterns at issue are not illnesses at all but other forms of deviance from technological society's current definition of normal as productive, other researchers continue to highlight the impossibility of disentangling the physical and the psychic in the single complex reality of the human person. Meanwhile the Roman Catholic Church in the United States has decided in favor of seeing this experience as illness by pronouncing at least some sufferers of serious mental illness suitable candidates for the anointing of the sick (PCS 53). Mary Frances Duffy extends this border creatively to include those who are facing the emotional and physical changes of midlife, which is its own kind of encounter with mortality in our contemporary culture. Beyond it lie the cases of those whose worlds have been devastated by loss not related to illness, such as economic misfortune, death, divorce, or any of the other threats which haunt us. Still farther beyond lie the cases of those whose worlds have been fragmented not through loss but through the personal choices of alienation to which we give the name sin.

Is it appropriate to respond ritually in the same way to each of these experiences of fragmentation, regardless of its cause? One question seems to be whether rites predicated upon the need for the restitution of relational worlds shattered in the confrontation with mortality specific to bodily illness can adequately embrace the need for relational reintegration in other experiences which follow a similar pattern of encounter with limit, loss of the future, and consequent disruption of world. It is true that every human experience of limit and consequent loss closes off the expected future, however momentarily. In this sense every limit experience is a symbolic encounter with death as the ultimate limit. However, it is equally true that there is an intimate and explicit correlation between sickness and death as manifestations of human mortality, which does not seem to exist in the case of other limit loss experiences. A second question seems to be whether rites predicated on the experiential pattern of limit, loss of future, and consequent fragmentation of world can appropriately address the experiences of fragmentation which do not appear to be engendered by a limit loss experience.

At root the question appears to be whether the Church's rites of healing, if they become so generalized as to address every experience of limit-loss or fragmentation, will continue to offer the particular integration of images of cure, reconciliation, and eschatological healing appropriate to those whose lives are disrupted by bodily illness itself. It would seem that rites which attempt to include every meaning risk losing all meaning. The tradition of sacramental diversity found in the Catholic Church suggests a different wisdom. While the Church celebrates Eucharist as the one comprehensive rite of eschatological healing in every human paschal experience, the Church also has always celebrated distinct rites of eschatological reconciliation for such experiences of fragmentation as sin, sickness, and bereavement. We acknowledge theologically that every form of division is a manifestation of evil, and therefore all forms of division are interrelated. Therefore we might expect a certain kinship among the rites addressed to each of these experiences. Moreover it is not always possible in the arena of pastoral reality to draw definitive lines. The question of rites appropriate to the mentally ill remains particularly difficult to resolve. However, we should take care with our rites of healing, lest in stretching them too wide, we see them snap in our hands, and their potential for speaking a healing word to any real human experience drain away to nothing.

Conclusion

We have come a long way from that Thursday afternoon drive along the interstate. We never did reach that meeting. We have wandered instead down the dark corridors of sickness, where we have found worlds in ruin. We have dared to look to the end of the tunnel, where we have seen death grinning behind the thin veil of sickness to make a mockery of the lives we had so treasured. Yet we have seen more. We have watched the Christian imagination of the future articulated in works of cure and reconciliation against the backdrop of the reign of God, boldly proclaimed in the Gospel and in rites as the age to come now made present in Jesus Christ. We have discovered a new world of meaning offered for our appropriation in the name of the one in whom death is itself undone by life. So we continue to gather in ritual assembly to confront the destructive presence of sickness in our midst with the hope that enlivens us:

> I saw the holy city, new Jerusalem. . . . I heard a loud voice proclaiming from the throne: 'Now God at last has a dwelling among people! God will dwell among them and they shall be God's people, and God will be with them. God will wipe away every tear from their eyes; there shall be an end to death, and to mourning and crying and pain; for the old order has passed away!' . . . Then the angel showed me the river of the water of life, sparkling like crystal, flowing from the throne of God and of the Lamb down the middle of the city's streets. On either side of the river stood a tree of life, which yields twelve crops of fruit, one for each month of the year; and the leaves of the tree are for the healing of the nations (Rev 21:3-4; 22:1-2).

References

Rituals Cited

"Ministration to the Sick." *The Book of Common Prayer.* San Francisco: Seabury Press, 1979.

Pastoral Care of the Sick. Collegeville, Minn.: The Liturgical Press, 1983.
"Service of the Word for Healing." *Occasional Services.* Minneapolis: Augsburg, 1982.
"The Office of Holy Unction." *Service Book of the Holy Orthodox-Catholic Apostolic Church,* trans. Isabel Florence Hapgood. Englewood, N.J.: Antiochian Orthodox Christian Archdiocese of New York and All North America, 1975.

Selected Reading

Becker, Ernest. *The Birth and Death of Meaning: A Perspective in Psychiatry and Anthropology.* New York: The Free Press, 1962. In this work, less popular than his *The Denial of Death,* Becker explores the symbolic nature of humanity as being-unto-meaning.
Berg, J. H. van den. *The Psychology of the Sickbed.* Pittsburgh: Duquesne University Press, 1966.
Cassell, Eric J. "Dying in a Technological Society," in *Death Inside Out: The Hastings Center Report.* Steinfels, Peter, and Veatch, Robert M., eds. New York: Harper & Row, 9–24.
Duffy, Regis. *A Roman Catholic Theology of Pastoral Care.* Philadelphia: Fortress Press, 1983. Taking a key insight from *The Rite for the Christian Initiation of Adults,* Duffy posits that all ministry exercised in the name of Jesus Christ, including ministry to the sick, has conversion as its ultimate goal.
Glen, M. Jennifer. "Sickness and Symbol: The Promise of the Future," *Worship* 54 (1980) 397–403. Some of the ideas developed in this chapter first appeared in this article on the anointing of the sick as rite of passage.
Grainger, Roger. *The Language of the Rite.* London: Darton, Longman & Todd, 1974. In this classic work, which undergirds the reflections on ritual in this chapter, Grainger explores the essentially relational nature of ritual.
Gusmer, Charles. *And You Visited Me: Sacramental Ministry to the Sick and Dying.* New York: Pueblo, 1984. This commentary on the Roman Catholic ritual, *Pastoral Care of the Sick,* describes the history and content of the revised rites for the sick and reflects on the theological, liturgical, and pastoral issues attendant upon them.
Holmes, Urban T. *Ministry and Imagination.* San Francisco: Seabury Press, 1976.
Israel, Martin. *Healing as Sacrament.* Cambridge, Mass.: Cowley Books, 1984. The author, a medical practitioner and Anglican priest, reflects on the significance of sickness and healing within a holistic eschatology.
Knauber, Adolf. *Pastoral Theology of the Anointing of the Sick,* trans. Matthew J. O'Connell. Collegeville, Minn.: The Liturgical Press, 1975.
Kübler-Ross, Elisabeth. *On Death and Dying.* New York: Macmillan, 1969.
Lane, Dermot. "The Activity of Faith," in *The Experience of God.* Ramsey, N.J.: Paulist Press, 1981, 51–71. Lane summarizes the work of key religionists and theologians on the nature of faith.
Lynch, William F. *Images of Hope.* Notre Dame, Ind.: University of Notre Dame Press, 1974. Lynch's study, pivotal to this chapter, examines the communal and imaginative nature of hope as a projection of the future and studies its converse, hopelessness, in the specific context of mental illness.

Parsons, Talcott. "Definitions of Health and Illness in the Light of American Values and Social Structures," in Jaco, E. Gartley, ed. *Patients, Physicians and Illness.* 2nd ed. New York: The Free Press, 1972. Parsons plays a key role in articulating the sociological concept of the sick role.

Perrin, Norman. *Jesus and the Language of the Kingdom.* Philadelphia: Fortress Press, 1976.

Power, David. "Let the Sick Man Call," *Heythrop Journal* 19 (1978) 256–270. In this article Power develops the concept of the sacramentality of the sick.

Rahner, Karl. *The Anointing of the Sick,* trans. Dorothy White. Denville, N.J.: Dimension Books, 1970.

Rahner, Karl. "Priest and Poet," in *Theological Investigations,* vol. II, trans. Karl-H. and Boniface Kruger. Baltimore: Helicon Press, 1967, 294–307. Rahner here muses on the power of poetic language, with reference to what he calls the "great words."

Szasz, Thomas. *The Myth of Mental Illness.* Revised ed. New York: Harper & Row, 1974. Szasz, a psychiatrist, is among those who challenge the appropriateness of illness as an image for nonnormative interpretations of reality.

Talley, Thomas. "Healing: Sacrament or Charism?" *Worship* 46 (1972) 518–552.

3. HISTORY OF ANOINTING AND HEALING IN THE CHURCH

Walter H. Cuenin

The history of the sacrament of the anointing of the sick is varied and at times difficult to trace. Many historical studies have already been written.[1] The purpose of this brief review is not to repeat that serious research. Rather, the reason for looking, however briefly, into this complicated history is to attempt to discern some clues which might be helpful in delineating future alternatives for the sacrament. In reflecting on the various changes that have taken place in the history of this sacrament and in trying to notice why those changes came about, one may be able to understand some of the significant aspects of the sacrament that could be critical to any planning for future directions.

In order to make some sense of a difficult and often convoluted history, I have chosen to develop this brief review in periods which reflect some of the more significant developments that have taken place in regard to the sacrament of anointing. These are Judeo-Christian beginnings, the first eight hundred years, the Carolingian reforms, the Scholastic period, and the period from the Council of Trent to the Second Vatican Council.[2]

Judeo-Christian Beginnings

The existence of a ritual for the anointing of the sick is not surprising when one considers that Christian faith has its roots in the Judeo tradition. The use of oil for anointing is attested to in the Jewish Scriptures. The laying on of hands and rituals of prayer for healing were a common part of the Palestinian scene. As with all the other ritual traditions of Christianity, we do not see evidence of the creation of entirely new forms. Rather, Jesus and the disciples simply took what they were familiar with and gave those prayer traditions new meaning in terms of their faith. In fact the tradition of a ritual involving oil and anointing probably predates Judaism. It seems as if these traditions were already deeply rooted in the Mediterranean world and probably reflect both good human instinct into the need for healing rituals and the significant place that olive oil has in the life of that region.

Therefore when we look at Jesus we need not be surprised that he saw healing the sick as a significant part of his ministry. It is not clear from the Scriptures whether or not Jesus himself engaged in a ministry of healing that involved anointing with oil. But this cannot be excluded either. It is fairly certain from texts such as Mark 6:13 that the disciples used oil in their ministry of healing.

The real significance of Jesus' healing, however, cannot be found in whether or not he used oil in anointing but rather in the total framework of his mission of proclaiming the coming of the kingdom of God. Jesus saw his healing the sick as a manifestation of God's power breaking through in the world. It was a sign that the victory of God's goodness over the power of evil as seen in human sickness was finally being made obvious to the world. His healing miracles were an important addition to this preaching of the good news. What is important for this chapter is that in the experience of Jesus, healing the sick was a vital link to the proclamation of God's power. That the disciples continued this healing in his name and used oil to anoint the sick as a sign of this transforming power indicate that the foundation of an ongoing healing ministry or ritual was established in the community directly from the experience of Jesus himself.

This connection of the rites of healing to Jesus and the apostolic Church has long been understood in the Church. Even the Council of Trent seemed to lean in this direction when it stated: "This sacred anointing of the sick was instituted by Christ our Lord as a true and proper sacrament of the New Testament. It is alluded to indeed by Mark (6:13), but it is recommended to the faithful and promulgated by James" (DS 1695). The epistle of James is often cited as the classic foundational text with regard to the sacrament of the anointing of the sick. It is perhaps more accurate to view it as a testimony to the early evidence of a healing ministry in the Church.

Nevertheless, when one looks at the early beginnings of the anointing of the sick, one is impressed by the attention given to these healing rituals and to the place of the sacred oil reserved for that purpose. This importance would continue at other periods of the Church's history, but it would change and develop for a variety of reasons. In noting these changes one will be able to discern the patterns and directions that might be useful in developing alternative rituals.

The First Eight Hundred Years

The evidence of the practice of the anointing of the sick is at best fragmentary. The principal sources for documentation are the texts for the blessing of the oil. *The Apostolic Tradition* of Hippolytus of 215 is perhaps the most significant witness:

> God who sanctifiest this oil, as Thou dost grant unto all who are anointed and receive of it the hallowing wherewith Thou didst anoint kings and priests and prophets, so grant that it may give strength to all that taste of it and health to all that use it.[3]

From this text it can be noted that the oil in question was intended for both application on the body and for drinking.

As was the custom in the early Roman Church, the faithful would not only bring the Eucharist home for weekly Communion, they would also take the blessed oil for their use when needed. There is no evidence of a presbyteral anointing at this time. The main thrust of the ritual evidence lies in the emphasis and importance that the early Church placed on the bishop's blessing of the oil. It was the sacred oil itself that seemed to have real importance. The manner of its application and use was not of particular significance as far as we can tell from the remaining evidence.

The first important reference to the practice of anointing the sick involving the ministration of the clergy can be noted in the often quoted letter of Pope Innocent to Decentius, the Bishop of Gubbio, in the fifth century. Innocent is speaking in reference to the text of the epistle of James:

> Now there is no doubt that these words are to be understood of the faithful who are sick and who can be anointed with the holy oil of chrism, which has been prepared by the bishop, and which not only priests but all Christians may use for anointing when their own needs or those of their family demand.

In answer to a question concerning the minister of the anointing, Pope Innocent writes:

If the bishop either can, or deems it proper that he should, visit someone in person, surely he whose office it is to prepare chrism can both
bless and anoint with chrism. But he can not pour it on penitents,
since it is a kind of sacrament. And how can it be deemed proper to
grant one kind of sacrament to those who are denied the rest of the
sacraments?[4]

These passages, although not a systematic treatment of the practice of the anointing of the sick, indicate that the anointing of the
sick was a common enough practice and that there was the possibility of some involvement by the clergy. The evidence seems clear
that anointing of the sick was common and the oil had to be blessed
by the bishop. The ministers of this anointing probably remained
for the most part the faithful.

As the Church continued to encounter other problems in regard
to dealing with the sick, one notices that more and more there
seemed to be a tendency to urge the faithful to seek recourse to the
Church and its ministers. This seems to be connected with a desire
to want to help the faithful avoid seeking the magical ministrations
of local healers, a practice which seemed inimical to the faith. This
stress on the value of the Church and the Church's oil may have
helped lead the way for a true presbyteral ritual which would only
become clear in the time of the Carolingian reforms.

This first period of the Church's history is characterized as a
time in which the practice of the anointing of the sick remained a
strong element in the life of the faithful. However, the involvement
of the Church community was minimal. The most important aspect
of this period is the strong insistence on the bishop's blessing of the
oil. Through that blessing the oil itself seemed to be the real sacrament. It had a sacred power of its own to help in the healing of
the sick.

The Carolingian Reforms

One of the chief characteristics of the Carolingian period was
its strong emphasis on the value of priestly ministry. From about
the year 800 on one can notice a marked shift of emphasis in the
sacramental life of the Church. The focus of many of the rituals
begins to move toward the role of the minister and his sacred power
in the ritual. This is particularly true of the ritual for the anointing
of the sick.

The concern of this chapter is not so much that it began to take
on a new emphasis but why that happened. In this period one be-

gan to observe the development of private penance and the end of canonical penance. With that came a greater tendency to administer sacramental penance at death.[5] Since this involved the priest, it also became more and more customary to use this time for the anointing of the person as well. With this association of anointing and deathbed reconciliation, a very important shift in the meaning of the anointing began to take shape. It gradually became more and more associated with the deathbed healing of the soul rather than its original association with the healing of the body.

Thus the increasing presbyteral anointing, when connected to the practice of deathbed reconciliation, made for a radical shift in the understanding of this sacrament. It was now on its way to becoming the last or "extreme" unction—the last anointing.

The Scholastic Period

The Scholastic period, marked as it was by its serious attempts to define and explain, attempted to understand the sacrament of anointing as it was known at that time. The ritual was by this point in history almost exclusively associated with death, so it is not surprising that when the Schoolmen went about the task of defining the effects of the sacrament, they would do so from that perspective.

In the earliest part of the Scholastic period, one can see that both bodily healing and spiritual healing are discussed as the effects of healing. This can be noted clearly in a text from Hugh of St. Victor written in 1141 in which he comments on the Epistle of James:

Hence it is clear that he who receives this anointing faithfully and with devotion unquestionably merits to receive through its alleviation and consolation both in body and soul, provided, however, that it is expedient that he be alleviated in both.[6]

Yet, during this period it became more and more customary to view the purpose of the anointing of the sick as an anointing for eternal life. The witness of William of Auvergne is important as a summation of the standard understanding of this sacrament in the Scholastic period:

Now since those who are departing this world are soon to be presented to God, it is not proper to doubt that they are to be sanctified from those faults which have clung to them while in this world, just as dust clings to the feet of the wayfarer, and from those slight and daily blemishes which are usually called venial sins.[7]

In this quote one can see how the practice of the anointing is now clearly seen as a spiritual cleansing of sins before death rather than as a ritual involved with the healing of the body. One of the major problems that emerged from this discussion concerned the bodily effect of the anointing. After all in the minds of the Scholastics, if sacraments are a means of grace, then how can an effect of a sacrament be bodily healing? Sacraments have to do with a supernatural grace. This type of theologizing, based in part on the actual experience that they had of the anointing associated with death, helped solidify the tradition of the sacrament as a type of final unction—an anointing for eternal glory.

From the Council of Trent to the Second Vatican Council

The most significant fact to be noted from the Tridentine period is that although heavily influenced by the Scholastic tradition and in reaction to the reformers who tended to eliminate this sacrament, the fathers of the Council of Trent did not completely endorse the theology of anointing as a spiritual reality. The Council stated that the effect of the sacrament is not simply the forgiveness of sins in preparation for eternal life but rather phrased it more globally as the gift of the Holy Spirit which has as its purpose the healing of the whole person—body, soul, and mind.

While in popular imagination the sacrament remained almost exclusively the sacrament for those dying, the official teaching of the Church was not so restrictive. Even in the midst of this popular understanding, the Church always tried to encourage people to receive the anointing before they were too close to death to be able to appreciate what was happening. This direction finally came to the fore when at the Second Vatican Council the Church fathers urged that the name of the sacrament be changed and that it reflect more carefully the ancient tradition. Viaticum was restored as the true sacrament for the dying, and the anointing of the sick was restored as a sacrament for those seriously ill even if not at the point of death.

Thus with the Second Vatican Council the Church witnessed an almost complete turnaround in a history that had moved from a simple concern for bodily healing in the early community to a ritual designed for spiritual healing at the time of death. This council most significantly restored the sacrament as an expression of Christ's healing power and concern for *all* who are sick.

In a history such as this, what is really important is not so much the exact outlines of the changes undergone by the ritual but the reasons which prompted the changes and which inspired each generation to approach the ritual in its own manner. Those reasons indicate some of the issues that have surfaced throughout history that allow today's Church to learn what may be necessary to consider for developing future rituals that will speak to Christians in the years that lie ahead.

Reflection on five such issues will conclude this chapter. Before that, however, it may be helpful to bring these historical notes into dialogue with some of the items raised by Orlo Strunk and Jennifer Glen. As I mentioned at the beginning of this historical sketch, the principal reason for presenting it here has not been simply to repeat historical studies already completed and readily available. Nor has it been to provide an indepth study of the sacrament's history. Rather, it was to provide a context from which to reflect on the ritual as it integrates human experience and to offer some future ritual projections. It is important, therefore, at least to note some of the concerns raised earlier in the chapters drawn from the human sciences and pastoral theology to see if and how those concerns were reflected and dealt with as the history of anointing and healing unfolded in the life of the Church.

At least four issues have been named by Strunk and Glen as issues for the present and future ministry of the Church on behalf of the sick: the individual and human sickness, the impact on the family of the sick person, the faith context of the sacrament, and sickness as an experience of evil.

The Individual and Human Sickness

In any presentation of the sacrament of the anointing of the sick, there could be a danger of forgetting that it is not the illness but the person who is ill who remains the primary focus of the sacrament. For that person especially sickness is not the issue, but rather that he or she is sick.

The Church's rituals themselves speak to the reality of sickness, but the word that is spoken is addressed to people who appropriate the experience of sickness and its meaning depending on many personal factors, such as background, experience, level of faith, and age. The sick are not simply "the sick." They are sick people, each with his or her unique qualities, strengths, and limitations.

The function of healing rituals is, therefore, not only to meet the felt religious needs that arise during sickness, but to speak to the sick person as he or she is experiencing the illness. The difficulty is that the ritual texts themselves, as presented in ritual books, do not always indicate that priority, nor do they always seem to make room for the vast range of varied experiences that Strunk so carefully outlined. To find illustrations of this kind of personal attention, which is in fact quite amply attested to in the history of the Catholic Church, one must look beyond the ritual to the traditions and patterns of healing prayer that are the stuff of so many Christian shrines and pilgrimages. These, one may say, filled the gap created by removing the anointing from all but the dying.

The most obvious example of this "living ritual" of healing is the shrine located at Lourdes, France. In modern times there is no shrine in the Christian world that has attracted as much attention or interest as has Lourdes. The scientific analyses of the various healings that have taken place there have been extraordinary. However one might choose to explain the healing, it is beyond any doubt that healing of the sick does occur at Lourdes.

What is important for this discussion is to notice how the focus of healing at Lourdes is very much directed to the individual and the particular sickness. Before a person actually enters the miraculous bath, that person has usually been significantly involved in a process that has been focused on curing a *particular* illness. For example in going to Lourdes, one goes for the cure of a cancer. One does not just go for general healing. It is this intense focus on the individual and the particular illness that gives the power to the Lourdes experience. Even those who are not cured testify to a tremendous transformation of faith that helps them live with the particular illness in a way that would not have been possible without the Lourdes experience.

A healing tradition such as Lourdes is an important witness to the presence in the Church of other systems of healing apart from the official sacrament of the anointing of the sick and in turn signals a need to which the future evolution of the sacrament must attend.

It would seem that this type of healing tradition suggests that in the Church one needs always to be attentive to the ways in which rituals work and do not work. Even with a tradition of the sacrament of the anointing, it has always been felt necessary to allow other healing experiences that enable an individual person to be more specifically attentive to his or her illness, rather than simply the general concerns that affect everyone who is ill.

The more recent development of the charismatic healing movement is also an example of how an individual's need to deal with illness is being met. Many people who may also participate in the sacrament of the anointing also find it helpful to be prayed over for a particular reason or to have some part of their body anointed and blessed at a healing service. Many congregations are developing regular healing services which may or may not involve the sacrament of the anointing. People are finding these important in the overall picture of healing.

The Impact on the Family of the Sick Person

One of the most profound realities of sickness is that it affects even those who are not ill. When a member of a family is ill, all in the family are affected by the illness. In some cases this can lead to exaggerated forms of exclusion and distrust from the wider community. For example, when a family member has AIDS, there often are fears that everyone in the house is contagious and therefore should be avoided. This is a stark and frightening example of the power of sickness to "infect" not only the sick person but the family and social network of the person.

The historical research on the sacrament of the anointing of the sick helps us to be aware of how this has been accomplished in the past. The whole initial period of the Church's history has shown that the key to the anointing was the anointing done by the family members themselves. Priestly anointing developed later. While psychological studies are not available, it is obvious that the participation of family members in bringing the oil to the home, making an offering for the oil, keeping the oil, and applying it frequently during the course of the illness must have been a powerful experience of bonding for the family. One may be powerfully ministered to by being minister.

In addition to that tradition popular customs such as lighting candles in the homes of the ill, placing a statue that is important to the family in the center of the house, and making special devotions together during the time of illness have helped family members deal with the stark reality of sickness in their midst. These customs of popular piety have been an important complement to the official ministrations of the Church in helping other family members integrate the experience of having one of their own be ill.

The Faith Context of the Sacrament

Usually when one thinks of the faith context of the sacrament one turns to the ritual itself. That is true, but only partially. It is also important to note how rituals are experienced and how the whole society or community understands the reality dealt with in the ritual. The sacrament of the anointing of the sick is an ongoing testament to the Church's concern to offer a way for its members to deal with sickness in light of the reality of Jesus Christ. However, there are other ways in which that faith context for illness has been developed that are important to attend to.

The long tradition in the Church of building hospitals and requiring wealthy people to provide places for the poor who were ill was a very significant way of maintaining a faith context for illness even when the sacrament of the anointing had become almost entirely associated with death. That is a communal statement to the importance of faith impacting on the reality of illness. One has but to think of the great healing institutions like Santo Spirito Hospital in Rome, founded in the ninth century for English pilgrims, to appreciate how important the whole faith context was for dealing with illness. The existence of these large hospices provided a means for the community to proclaim, even through their buildings, that sickness was a reality that entered into the fabric of faith. It was a way of saying a word of meaning to the harsh reality of sickness apart from the ritual. The presence in more recent times of large numbers of religious communities of men and women devoted to caring for the sick is another example of how the Church has sought to offer a context of faith to the reality of sickness. These communities may be as important as any ritual for what they say to the whole fabric of meaning in the Church. Their existence is an affirmation of hope apart from the context of the ritual.

Sickness as an Experience of Evil

One of the observations made by social scientists concerning illness is that it is a harsh reality which needs to be dealt with directly and not denied. Denial of the evil of sickness is a problem of tremendous proportions in today's society where illness is relegated largely to the hospital. In the past this was not a major problem, because sickness was experienced more in the midst of a living family. Being close to it forced everyone to see the ugliness and pain that goes with sickness. Antiseptic hospitals often mask the grimness of disease, and drugs often tranquilize the sick so that pain is minimal. However, in dealing with illness from a faith perspective, it is important not to forget the horrendous power of sickness to destroy our bodies, minds, and spirits.

This has always been addressed in the Church by the very way in which the rituals were conducted. They involved physical touching of the body, which put the believer into contact with the contagion. This very real touching of the sick allowed people to deal directly with illness and to experience it as evil. Holding a vigil around a sick person until death and continuing to reverence the body after death in the home also afforded people an opportunity through their faith traditions to have immediate contact with human sickness. It is important that this lesson from the history of the Church not be lost.

These four areas are not exhaustive. Rather, they highlight the importance of the studies of the social sciences for a true understanding of religious ritual. As seen in this brief historical review, each of the concerns of the social scientists reflects an insight into the human person's struggle to deal with illness. The sacrament of the anointing of the sick is a part of a larger tradition that attempts to face the reality of sickness with the hopeful message of the Gospel of Jesus Christ.

We have reviewed a brief history of the sacrament of the sick and reflected in dialogue with the human sciences how issues throughout history have been met, albeit not always successfully and not always in ways associated with the sacrament strictly speaking. This final section points us in the direction of alternative futures for the sacrament. Some areas that need to be assessed are: the minister of the sacrament, the value of presbyteral anointing, the reason for the sacrament, the connection of the sacrament to reconciliation, and oil as a medium of healing.

The Minister of the Sacrament

One of the most obvious facts observed in any review of the history of this sacrament is that the role of the clergy in the anointing was rather late in coming. While we do not know for certain that the clergy were not involved in early days, the overwhelming evidence would indicate that the role of the clergy was at best minimal.

The custom of the laity taking the blessed oil to their homes for their own use seems by far to be the dominant practice at least for about eight hundred years. This has to have serious impact on any contemporary scholarship concerned with this sacrament. Although later generations of the Church might associate this sacrament with the epistle of James and thereby see in that passage a kind of divine warrant for the use of the clergy in the anointing, the broader view of history is that the epistle of James did not have that effect on the first eight hundred years of the Church's history.

This historical review makes it clear that one cannot simply look at the epistle of James and use that passage anachronistically to justify the practice of clerical anointing, which did in fact become the customary way in the Church. The passage itself does not necessarily answer today's questions concerning the minister of the sacrament. Since in fact the Church has experienced a variety of ways of administering this sacrament, that seems to be one of the most significant points that history can show us for today's Church.

Clearly the question of who should administer the sacrament is a major issue in contemporary sacramental theology. In a Church in which the pastoral ministry to the sick and elderly is increasingly performed by nonordained ministers or by deacons, there is developing a sense that these persons who perform the pastoral ministry should also be the ones who are entitled to administer the Church's rituals for healing. After all, good sacramental theory demands some real connection between the minister and the community. This applies not only to the faith community that would gather around a sick person for the anointing but also to the minister who leads the ritual of healing and who must be an integral part of that community. What sense does it make to bring in a priest from "outside," who may have little or no contact with the sick person and the family, to perform a ritual which is intended to be celebrated within a community that presumes some knowledge of the persons engaged in the ritual? In some ways this is similar to the dilemma faced by the Church in the area of sacramental reconciliation. With the work of reconciliation more and more entrusted to men and women who are not ordained, it must be asked how we can incorporate that true reconciliation with the official sacramental reconciliation of the Church. In that sacrament the issue is more challenging because of the stronger connection between ordination and the ministry of forgiving sins. But in the case of the anointing of the sick, the Church itself has seen other models. It might be that now is the time to begin exploring the possibility of others than the ordained being given the mandate to celebrate this sacrament.

Another way to approach this issue might be to consider the development of healing rituals that could be celebrated by lay persons and other ministers that could complement the official ministry of the Church. As penitential services that do not include sacramental reconciliation are found in the ritual for the forgiveness of sins, so one might conceive in future rituals the possibility of a celebration for the sick that would not include the sacramental anointing. However, one still needs to wonder whether these "extra" sacramental services are strictly speaking "extra" sacramental. What will be the actual experience of them by the people involved? It may well be that where nonsacramental but truly meaningful healing services are celebrated, the official sacramental ritual might appear to be redundant. In point of fact, however, if we may draw from the experience of reconciliation again, penitential services without sacramental reconciliation have not been popular. They seem to lack "the real thing." This may also happen with anointing.

On the other hand, it may prove more helpful to go the way of developing these healing rituals rather than spending a lot of energy on whether the Church should officially change its position on the minister of the sacrament. Thus in any future alternative forms of healing rituals, one of the key factors will be attention to the development of prayer forms that allow the actual ministers of pastoral healing to be the leaders of the ritual. The connection between the minister who leads the worship and the minister who does the pastoral ministry should be maintained. The history of the Church should show us that there is no real theological problem with this, since in fact the minister of the sacrament was for so long a time a family member of the sick person.

It is interesting to note how lay persons have in fact been involved in healing rituals. This becomes noticeable when one considers the importance throughout history of the use of blessed oils from the shrines of various saints. Many pilgrimages have been made to various healing shrines, and the people brought home the oil that they either drank or applied to their own bodies. It seems almost that when the official sacrament became exclusively a ritual administered by the priest, the people maintained a parallel tradition. These more obscure notes from our history should not be neglected, however, because they show the richness of the actual experience of the people.

The Value of Presbyteral Anointing

The other side of this history is that for almost twelve hundred years presbyteral anointing of the sick has been the norm. Although it is not possible to speculate on the frequency with which the sacrament was administered in much of this time span, nevertheless, there does seem to be something to note in the custom of the presbyteral anointing.

While the requirement for presbyteral anointing stems more from the connection of this sacrament to deathbed reconciliation, nevertheless, there is a value to be taken from this tradition as we consider future options. The value of the presbyteral anointing lies not so much in the fact that the minister is ordained as in what ordination means and how that makes this link understandable.

The ordained minister is by virtue of place in the life of the community the leader. As leader of a local community, that person would want to take an active role in any efforts of the community to reach out to those who are sick. The history of presbyteral anointing indicates that the connection of the sacrament of anointing to those who lead the community has merit. In any future option for ritual development, this connection between presidency over a community—signified in ordination—and presidency over the rituals of healing needs to be seriously considered.

The Reason for the Sacrament

The history of the sacrament of anointing reveals that the ritual has taken on a variety of meanings throughout the life of the Church. At times bodily healing was primary; at other times spiritual healing was more important. Still again for a long time the sacrament was viewed almost exclusively as a final preparation for death. This multiplicity of reasons for the existence of the sacrament indicates a need for any future ritual to be concerned about the raison d'etre of the ritual. It is not sufficient to create alternative rituals without first wondering what is the intended purpose of the ritual being developed.

It would seem that we need to be careful not to structure any future ritual too closely. It is often wise to allow for a multiplicity of meanings even in the same celebration. The healing of the body never seems to have been the only focus given to healing in our tradition. While bodily healing was being prayed for, there has always been a sense that the real healing lies within the person and involves a deeper level of meaning beyond bodily healing. Thus in future rituals, attending to the variety of meanings is the key. A person who is sick needs a ritual of healing, not so much for bodily healing as for the sense of meaning that the ritual provides the sick person to deal with the illness and its devastating effects. The meaning behind any healing ritual developed in the Christian community goes well beyond the healing of the body. This needs to be mentioned carefully since there is developing in the Church a much keener awareness of the sacrament as a sacrament for human sickness.

This becomes especially true in a highly technological society in which so much of the bodily healing is done in hospitals. However, as mentioned before, this medical treatment rarely attends to the deeper issues that are raised by sickness. Healing rituals of the Church have the potential to be ways in which seriously ill persons can begin to develop a horizon of meaning to make sense out of an otherwise desperate situation.

Since the Second Vatican Council there has been so much focus on the restoration of the sacrament of the anointing of the sick that one might get the impression that its main purpose is to be in competition with the medical community. This is not and should not seem to be the case. On the contrary, the best sacramental and pastoral ministry should work in cooperation with the efforts of contemporary medical research. Sacramental ministry contributes by altering the meaning of sickness. It will best achieve its role when it allows the full scope of that meaning to be heard, felt, and deeply embraced by the person being anointed.

The Connection of the Sacrament to Reconciliation

From the history presented one notes that for a long period of the Church's experience the anointing of the sick was associated with deathbed reconciliation. In fact the sacrament of anointing came more and more to be associated almost exclusively with the forgiveness of sins or the punishments due to them rather than a ritual that had to do with healing of the body.

This association may be of some value in this discussion of future alternatives for this sacrament. The association of anointing of the sick with the forgiveness of sins does tend to highlight something that may be too easily overlooked in today's Church, the connection of serious illness to the reality of sin.

No one would argue today that personal sin results in sickness. That is expressly denied in the introduction to the new anointing ritual. Nevertheless, there is a sense in which grave illness needs to be appreciated as a reflection of the evil in the world that is the result of sin. For many persons a serious illness still has intimations of dissolution and alienation. It is a frightening experience that often results in a loss of faith and can be felt as a true moment of evil.

The new rites of the Church may be a little too "clean" in their language dealing with the reality of illness. Would there not still be a place for referring to the driving out of Satan or of the "Evil One," because in fact people often perceive illness as if they had been taken over by some evil power?

Any alternative rituals will need to be able to deal with the dark side of sickness in a direct and yet poetic way that allows the human imagination the scope to face the evil and apply to it the deeper reality of the victory of Christ. By not tending adequately to this dark reality, one could run the risk of emasculating the ritual.

The historical link of the sacrament of anointing with reconciliation may well be viewed as at least a reminder that sickness is related to sin. It is not simply a question of developing healing rituals that focus exclusively on the healing of the body. Any new rituals will need to address the evil power of illness and thereby find words and gestures that will allow that evil to be dealt with. Some explicit mention and concern about this dark side of sickness needs to find a place in any new rituals.

Oil as a Medium of Healing

One constant throughout this brief history of the sacrament of the anointing of the sick is the place and prominence of oil. Whether administered by the laity or by a priest, the sacred oil always had a central part in the ritual. As noted this is understandable when one considers the place that oil had in the culture in which the first ecclesial rituals emerged.

This presents a serious challenge to contemporary liturgists. Does oil have similar meaning in today's world? Is there any real appreciation for the sacredness of oil? Our ritual minimalism of the last four hundred years has certainly obscured the consciousness of oil from the minds of most Catholics. Yet even with any restoration of oil to a position of prominence, is there any real appreciation for it? Is it a symbol that has been displaced?

It would seem that in any alternative rituals careful attention will need to be paid to this point. Perhaps with more focus on the oils in the everyday life of the Church and with a better use of the oil by the ministers in the actual anointing, the oil might begin to recover some of the significance that it had for other generations.

One thing is clear, however, from experience in pastoral minis-

try. The touch and the caress that go with the application probably have as big an impact as the use of blessed oil. The way in which
it is applied can be a moment of gentle reverence for a sick body
and does imbue the oil with a certain sacredness from the very person who is anointed.

Conclusion

As can be noted from this chapter, the history of the sacrament
of the anointing of the sick is rich and complicated. It does hold
some clues, however, as to components and patterns of ritual that
could be important in the development of future alternative rites.
The history does not give all the answers. The picture is too murky
for that. It does, however, suggest a direction or two. Following
those leads and sensitive to the ever-changing developments in the
medical field, healing rituals that speak to the contemporary person in the midst of serious illness can be created and effectively
celebrated.

Footnotes

1. Bernhard Poschmann, *Penance and the Anointing of the Sick* (New York,
Herder, 1963). Charles Gusmer, *And You Visited Me: Sacramental Ministry to
the Sick and Dying* (New York, Pueblo, 1984). There is an excellent bibliography
in this book.

2. The outline of historical periods used in this paper is taken from Gusmer's
book cited above.

3. *The Apostolic Tradition*, ed. Gregory Dix (London: SPCK, 1968) V, p. 10.

4. *Sacraments and Forgiveness. Sources of Christian Theology II*, ed. Paul
Palmer (Westminster, Md.: Newman Press, 1959) 283–284.

5. In addition to this connection of anointing to deathbed penance, there were
other factors that influenced the history of the sacrament and which contributed
to making it more and more removed from the experience of the people. The custom of paying the clergy for their services tended to encourage putting off the
ritual until the last possible moment. The popularity of local healing customs never
died out in the Church. Many people who were only marginally members of the
Church continued to use their own, more ancient methods of healing.

6. Paul Palmer, "The Purpose of Anointing the Sick: A Reappraisal," *Theological Studies* 19 (1958) 326.

7. *Ibid.* 331.

RITUALS

ALTERNATIVE 1: RITUAL OF ANOINTING FOR THE LONG-TERM, SERIOUSLY ILL

Gerald Calhoun, S.J., and Peter E. Fink, S.J.

Introduction

The revised Roman Ritual *Pastoral Care of the Sick* represents a wonderful recovery of the sacramental ministry of the Church toward the sick and the dying. The anointing of the sick as the Church's prayer of healing is restored to all the sick, and no longer restricted to those alone whose sickness takes them close to death's door. Restored too is the possibility of enacting this sacramental prayer several times during an illness, thus allowing the Church to be companion to the sick throughout the duration of their sickness. For the long-term, seriously ill, this frequent companionship is extremely important.

The alternative presented here seeks to capture this restored ability to repeat the healing sacrament in the course of an illness and to focus specifically on those whose illness is long, serious, and probably leading to life's end. More than simple repetition is at issue. If it were not, the revised *Pastoral Care of the Sick* would be adequate to the task. What is at issue for the long-term seriously ill is the *context* of the sacrament, which Orlo Strunk identified as a major factor in successful sacramental enactment. The *context* of the sacrament is shaped uniquely when one's illness is long and terminal.

Jennifer Glen has observed that a major contribution of the anointing sacrament is to provide some link with a "world remembered," that is, the world of the healthy which one has left. Because it provides this link, anointing can serve to counter the sense of isolation which sickness tends to induce. This is certainly true when the sickness is of relatively short duration and when such remembrance can itself be a healing factor, and indeed a source of hope. When the sickness is prolonged, however, and especially when there may be little expectation of a return to that world of the healthy, the world of the sick becomes itself *the major context*, and the community of the sick a far more important source of hope and healing than the remembered world of the healthy.

The ritual presented here aims to bring out from a community of the sick resources for hope and for healing. It is presented in two parts. The first is a pastoral essay by Gerald Calhoun which, while speaking about a ritual enactment of the sacrament, seeks to name something which ritual text alone cannot name. He describes the dimension of *presence* that is so essential to sacramental ministry to the sick, and all the more so when sickness is both prolonged and terminal. *Presence* here is threefold: of the minister to the sick, of the healthy to the sick, and most important of all, of the sick to the sick. The second part is a liturgical text by Peter Fink that tries to embody in ritual form this combined sense of presence.

Part I: A Pastoral Essay

I. PREPARATION

With seriously ill persons, whether they be victims of chronic, long-term diseases or suffer from fast-moving terminal illnesses, the pastoral relationship is the most significant factor in preparing for the celebration of the anointing of the sick. When the pastoral minister spends time getting to know the ill person and the person's family through regular visits, thus creating an atmosphere in which they can freely express all their reactions to their sickness and confinement, then the sacrament can address the particular emotional, interpersonal, and spiritual "states" of the people involved. If, for example, there is for the sick person and for the family a great deal of anger about the burden of this serious illness, sparking questions and doubts about God's love for them, a pastoral minister can respond personally to them and can bring their anger and questions into the prayers and readings of the sacrament itself. Whether the predominant reaction at any given time be one of denial, fear, guilt, anger, depression, hope, or a combination of feelings, personal knowledge of the persons to receive and participate in the anointing is a critical first step in preparing for a liturgical celebration.

To facilitate an experience of healing for seriously ill persons and for their families and for their caregivers, the sacrament of the sick needs to include their desires for physical, attitudinal, relational, and spiritual healing. In listening compassionately, then, to their responses to their struggles, pastoral ministers begin to recognize what are the most important pastoral needs. Perhaps those in denial need courage and strength; those in depression need hope; and those in guilt need forgiveness and peace. In preparing the specifics of celebrating the anointing of the sick, then, ministers can assure not only recognition of their reactions before God, but also supplication for and symbolic gestures of the desired gifts of the Spirit. Which Scripture texts are selected, how prayers are formulated, the focus of the homily, the ways people are encouraged to participate in the laying on of hands and in the prayers of the faithful—all of this preparation must take into careful consideration what type of healing the people seek, while always leaving room in the celebration for God to heal in other ways.

Because of the history of the sacrament in the Catholic community, many individuals with serious illnesses also need a pastoral catechesis in order to approach the sacrament with hope and not with fear. Disassociating the implications of "extreme unction" from the sacrament of the sick involves telling people directly that the Church has changed the emphasis from immediate preparation for death to a prayer and celebration of God's healing love. By adding that this is a sacrament for living and not just for dying frees people to ask for the strength and renewed faith offered by the anointing. Even though many Catholics have heard of the changes in emphasis in the sacrament of the sick, old associations and anxieties can surface spontaneously at the time of serious illness, causing the mention of the sacrament to heighten fear instead of promising peace. So, pastoral ministers must be explicit in reiterating the meaning of the anointing of the sick and must ask directly if the people involved want to receive it. Usually a brief explanation which is sensitive to their religious experience will prepare people to look forward to the sacrament, recognizing it as a time to pray for one another and to hear God's words of consolation.

Immediate preparation for celebrating the sacrament of the sick among seriously ill persons involves inviting the sick, their families, and, if possible, their caregivers to become participants in and not just observers of the anointing. By describing the celebration as a special moment for all of them to express their support of one another and to experience God's promise of healing for all of them, the pastoral minister can encourage them to enter actively into the liturgy of anointing. While there is no need for the pastoral minister to mention ahead of time the explicit ways of participating in the celebration of the sacrament, creating an atmosphere and an expectation of involvement helps the sick persons, the families, and the caregivers to identify their desires for healing and for God's strength before the actual celebration of the anointing.

II. CELEBRATION OF THE SACRAMENT

A. Communal Liturgies

When preparation for the anointing of the sick has been completed (in all but emergency situations), the pastoral minister(s) selects the most appropriate location and time for the celebration of the sacrament. If at all possible, usually the most beneficial setting for the anointing of a seriously ill person is in the context of a Eucharist together with other seriously ill individuals, their families, and their caregivers. A uniquely compassionate community among such people is highlighted and enhanced by a celebration of the sacrament in common; there is a certain communication of mutual understanding and shared faith that helps them support and pray for one another. Even if seriously ill persons are bedridden, it is well worth the effort of transporting them in bed to a chapel or a large room so that they can join others in similar conditions who seek the Lord's healing. Once they are all gathered together, arranging in a circle individual sick persons next to one another and with their families and caregivers close by will provide an atmosphere of physical and emotional intimacy. This gives all of the participants permission to remain attuned to one another before, during, and after the liturgical celebration.

Music that sets a desired mood or expresses the prayerful sentiments of the participants needs to be carefully selected. Creating a contemplative atmosphere before the liturgy begins by playing a meditative hymn or soft instrumental music usually prompts people to pay attention to what is happening inside themselves, as well as to become aware of the quiet companionship they share with one another. When followed by introductory remarks of welcome that invite people to bring their feelings, desires, and needs before the Lord, this soothing music at the start moves participants fairly easily and quickly into a relaxed and open stance before God.

After setting this contemplative tone, the celebrant of the Eucharist or some other appropriate person offers a brief explanation of the sacrament of the sick, focusing on the gift of healing in its various dimensions and describing the different aspects of the sacrament as they will unfold throughout the liturgy. In mentioning the laying on of hands, the anointing with oil, and the prayer of blessing at the conclusion of the liturgy, attention should be given to encouraging all the participants to pray for one another as well as for themselves.

The opening prayer before the Scripture readings provides the celebrant with an initial opportunity to express the community's desire for healing, while renewing its trust in God's promise to heal. Suggesting that the participants mention aloud how they want the Lord to heal them and to heal one another enables the celebrant to present all their specific hopes before the Lord and to ask in their behalf for the freedom to notice how God will choose to offer healing. Because most seriously ill persons have expanded their hopes for healing beyond the expectation of a physical cure, their prayers usually encompass petitions for relational, emotional, and spiritual healing. The opening prayer, then, can reiterate their willingness to let God continue to surprise them in their understanding and experience of healing.

The selection of appropriate Scripture readings for the particular seriously ill persons present and for their families and their caregivers will be suggested by the minister's personal knowledge of the participants in the context of their on-going pastoral relationships. Whether to emphasize protest about their illness or puzzlement over its purpose or helplessness before God or gratitude for the blessings of life or renewed trust in the Lord's promise of new life depends primarily upon pastoral awareness of individuals' faith journeys. In a communal celebration of the sacrament of the sick, ministers must choose Scripture readings that address these specific attitudes and responses toward God, while at the same time leaving the selections general enough to appeal to a variety of faith reactions. Fortunately there are many New Testament stories of Jesus offering God's healing love to individuals in varying circumstances, but always pointing them toward reconciliation in their relationships with self, with others, and with God. Most seriously ill persons and their families can identify in some significant ways with any of these healing encounters. Concrete stories, whether from the Old or the New Testament, which exemplify very human reactions to personal tragedy or misfortune, seem to speak most loudly to seriously ill persons of faith.

In the homily during a communal celebration of the sacrament of the sick, the preacher needs to draw connections between the participants' experience of their faith in the midst of critical illness and the Word of life spoken by Jesus. Because of peoples' emotional and religious backgrounds, there are certain emphases that ought to be explicitly affirmed: (1) that all the feelings experienced by the seriously ill are appropriate and acceptable to God, (2) that God in Jesus is compassionate, especially toward the sick, (3) that people are not losing their faith when they question God or voice negative feelings toward God, (4) that serious illness is often an experience of a changing and deepening faith, (5) that there are different forms of miracles that God invites them to notice in their lives, and (6) that each person, like Jesus, is challenged to learn to trust God in the face of personal suffering and death. These and other reminders in a homily for a liturgy of anointing seriously ill persons can help expand people's expectations of who God is and how to recognize God within their daily struggles with sickness and dying. Often a homilist can facilitate new discoveries of God as comforter to people in their sicknesses, laying the groundwork for them to notice signs of healing, new life, and resurrection in their very experiences of letting go and of dying. By stressing that God in Christ takes people wherever they are in their reactions to sickness and death and that the Lord keeps inviting them to have hope in God's faithfulness, the homilist leads the seriously ill to expect strengthening from their faith in God's compassion toward them.

After the Liturgy of the Word and the homily are concluded, the laying on of hands takes place, beginning with a brief explanation of this ancient symbol of invoking God's blessing. Since touch is extremely important for people who are ill, they readily welcome the connections between this gesture and the Lord's blessing and desire to heal them. Since much of their sense of God's presence to them during illness occurs in their caring for one another, it is also very natural to suggest that families hold the hands of their loved one or put their arms around the shoulders of the seriously ill person while others are imposing hands on the person's head. By slowly moving from person to person, while gently resting hands on their heads for several seconds, pastoral ministers help create a tangible experience of the Lord's presence.

Besides the pastoral ministers who are present, the celebrant can invite other caregivers and friends and relatives to lay their hands on the heads of the ill persons. While this is occurring, people should be asked to pray silently for one another that the Lord will bring about healing in whatever way each person needs. Quiet music or an appropriate hymn can be played in the background; (communal singing will usually distract from the poignancy of the laying on of hands.) Quite frequently this aspect of the sacrament of the sick produces deep emotions and tears from all the participants, a witness to the profound effect of being touched in the Lord's name.

After pausing for a short while to allow the impact of the laying on of hands to sink in, the celebrant can initiate the anointing itself by explaining in a few words the symbolism of anointing in the tradition of the Church. In this way participants not only begin to understand why oil is used in this sacrament, but may even request the celebrant to anoint the parts of their bodies where they are in pain or are diseased. Sometimes this request occurs spontaneously when the celebrant approaches a person for the traditional anointing on the forehead and on the palms of their hands. Because of the prayer for healing that accompanies this anointing, there should be no music so that all participants can listen to and affirm the prayer in their hearts. Knowing each participant individually through continuing pastoral relationships will allow the ministers who anoint to compose a prayer that addresses the particular needs and experiences of each seriously ill person. What type of healing each one seeks, how each one needs to be comforted by the Lord, and what words of strengthening would speak to each individual are considerations which the minister attends to in approaching the various participants. Encouraging the people who have been anointed to rub the oil into their hands (instead of having someone immediately wipe off the excess oil with cotton) reinforces the healing symbolism of the anointing. When the preparatory ministry and the just-completed Liturgy of the Word and the homily have carefully and sensitively attuned participants to the sacrament of the sick, then this actual anointing speaks very clearly as a powerful sign of Christ who is healing them and will continue to heal them.

As they move toward the Liturgy of the Eucharist after the anointing, expression of their prayers of the faithful are particularly appropriate, especially when participants are invited to pray for the needs of other people. This focus recalls the communal dimension of the sacrament of the sick and helps the seriously ill and their families to remember that they are part of a larger world and a larger Church. Since, contrary to popular belief, most persons facing serious and terminal illness remain interested in people, events, and places outside of themselves almost to the very end of their lives, their praying for others, especially those suffering in various ways, recognizes and reaffirms their participation in the community of all God's people. Consequently the offering of the gifts immediately following the prayers of the faithful opens up the seriously ill to join the Lord in presenting the cares and burdens of all their brothers and sisters before the Creator God.

Singing the various acclamations during the Eucharistic Prayer can provide the participants with a means of expressing their hope and their peace renewed by the anointing celebration. Probably even more than those who enjoy good health, seriously ill persons appreciate opportunities to sing and to listen to music; their spirits which are sometimes encumbered with many worries and fears are revived by the gift of music, especially in the context of worship and the sharing of their faith. Practicing simple acclamations before the liturgy or having them repeat an antiphon after a musician introduces it offers participants the chance to praise God in a heartfelt way.

If there is time and the ill persons do not appear to be too tired, the celebrant can invite individuals after Communion to mention briefly the blessings for which they want to thank God. This suggestion usually receives a ready welcome because participants feel relaxed and bonded to one another through the shared experience of the anointing and the Eucharist. After bringing all these prayers of gratitude to God, the celebrant can give thanks in the name of the community for the sacramental presence of Christ. Then the final blessing, calling for health and healing and hope, will capture for the seriously ill, their families, and their caregivers a deep sense that God who has blessed them in the past promises to be their companion in the future.

B. Individual Celebrations of the Sacrament of the Sick

When it is not possible to bring a particular seriously ill person together with others for a communal celebration of the sacrament of the sick, then the anointing can take place with a smaller group of people: the ill person, the family, and the caregivers. Usually this anointing will not be in the context of a Eucharist, although Communion may be given to the seriously ill person after the sacrament of the sick is celebrated. All the same considerations for a communal liturgy of the sacrament are applicable to an individual anointing. Preparation within a pastoral relationship, choosing the most appropriate time of celebration, active involvement by the seriously ill person, the family, and the caregivers in the prayers, readings, laying on of hands, and the prayers of the faithful remain as important for the anointing of one person as they are in communal celebrations.

Sometimes the intimacy of a single anointing allows participants to express their feelings and their faith more easily than within a large group. Pastoral ministers who have established close rapport with the individual participants can gently draw them out so that they begin to communicate to one another their deeper emotions and their most personal prayers. If, for example, some members of the family need reconciliation with the seriously ill person, they may be able to ask forgiveness of one another during the beginning of the celebration when the minister asks the participants how they seek healing from the Lord. Or if the celebrant suggests that the participants mention during the prayers of the faithful not only their concerns about others but also their sentiments of gratitude, the ill person and the family may relive together some of their precious memories. As they remember these shared moments of happiness and of suffering in the context of celebrating the sacrament of the sick, many people experience an affirmation of their love for one another and of God's love for them. By recognizing this type of grieving as part of the gift of healing, pastoral ministers encourage individuals and families to discover the Lord touching them in the heart of their human relationships.

Finally, in individual celebrations of the sacrament of the sick there is often more opportunity than in larger groups for the minister to tailor the readings, the prayers, and the homily to the pastoral needs of the particular family involved. This becomes especially significant when the sacrament is repeated periodically during the course of a progressive illness, because a minister can emphasize in each celebration the specific attitudes and reactions that are predominant at the time. Toward the beginning of a serious illness, for instance, when most people experience considerable anger and fear, the anointing may focus on assisting them to verbalize these feelings to God and to pray for understanding and strength. As the seriously ill person grows physically weaker and the family starts to grieve by reviewing their lives together, the celebration of the sacrament can highlight the providence of God in being a faithful companion to them over the years. Then toward the last stages of an illness which are usually characterized by an emerging peace about the life and relationships that have been shared, the sacrament of the sick can reinforce trust and hope in God's promises of new life as death approaches. With seriously ill persons and with their families, there is frequently a discernible process in their feelings and in their faith as they confront multiple losses and death itself. In determining the frequency and the timing of celebrations of the sacrament of the sick, pastoral ministers ought to take their cues from the various "stages" of the faith journeys encountered by individuals and by their families.

III. FOLLOW-UP MINISTRY

Just as important as preparation for anointing and the celebration of the sacrament itself is the on-going pastoral relationship that continues afterwards. Ministers often notice in conversations with seriously ill persons and with their families during the days following a liturgy of anointing that one of the effects of the sacrament can be a movement from one faith stance toward the illness to another; in other words, a grace of the sacrament may be to serve as a transition into a new and potentially more sustaining encounter with God. One such transition that can be precipitated by a sensitive celebration of the sacrament of the sick concerns an ill person's letting go of the need to understand why God allows her or him to experience a life-threatening illness and to concentrate instead on discovering how God is present in the midst of their suffering. In their follow-up visits after an anointing, pastoral ministers have a unique opportunity to affirm this transition as part of the Lord's healing through the sacrament and they can encourage the seriously ill person and the family to ask the Lord for what they now seek in facing the crisis of progressive illness. The role of the minister is then to help them to recognize the ways in which the Lord offers them healing in their daily struggles.

It sometimes happens that a celebration of anointing may heighten rather than resolve a person's faith dilemma. Direct expression of uncomfortable feeling reactions toward God, such as anger, guilt, helplessness, or fear, can surface after a liturgy of anointing, leaving people confused and in need of compassionate direction. A pastoral minister who has learned from experience to trust the process of faith throughout the progression of serious illness will be able to encourage people to face these uneasy feelings toward God, reassuring them that by being honest and direct they will eventually experience a deeper peace in their faith. In listening to and accepting these unsettling responses to God, ministers themselves can be signs of the Lord's healing love for the seriously ill and for their families.

The sacrament of the sick for persons facing serious and terminal illness is both a celebration of and a source of the healing power of Christ. What is highlighted by the anointing is the faithfulness of God to the ill person and the family, not only at the time of the sacrament but throughout the intense, day-to-day living with sickness and with dying. When this faithfulness is concretized and symbolized by the constancy of a pastoral relationship and by the steady care of family members for one another, then the preparation, the celebration, and the follow-up of the sacrament of the sick can be most effective in sensitizing everyone to the presence of Christ who wants to heal. Pastoral ministers among the seriously ill, therefore, who invite people to celebrate the anointing of the sick, offer a most credible witness to the meaning of the sacrament when they commit themselves to a compassionate companionship that mirrors the faithfulness of the Lord.

Part II: Ritual for Anointing the Long-Term Seriously Ill

This ritual is designed as a communal celebration of the sacrament of the anointing to take place within the context of a Eucharistic liturgy. Family, friends, and, if possible, caregivers are invited to gather with the seriously ill in a place suitable for worship. The *primary* community of worship, however, remains the ill persons themselves. Care should be taken that the liturgy not be celebrated in such a way that the sick persons become passive observers because of a pace set by the healthy. Care should be taken too that the sick persons gathered achieve some sense of relationship among themselves, and not simply with the cluster of their family and friends.

Introductory Rites

GATHERING

As the people gather in the space set aside for worship, music which is soft and inviting and yet which proclaims the presence and comfort of God should be playing. It may be recorded music or music sung by a small group of singers.

As the people gather, the presiding celebrant greets each of the sick in a personal manner and also welcomes the accompanying families and friends.

When all are gathered, the presiding celebrant and ministers go to the front and begin the service.

CALL TO WORSHIP

Presider: My brothers and sisters,
welcome to God's house.
I wish you peace and healing
and the deep strength of our common faith
in God and in Jesus Christ.

You who are sick especially
are honored guests in God's house.
And we who join you in prayer
are honored to be with you.

May the peace and blessing of God our Father
and the Lord Jesus Christ be with you.

All: And also with you.

The presider goes now to each of the sick and asks in these or similar words:

Presider: *N.*, as you come into God's presence this day,
what special prayer do you bring to God?

Each of the sick is invited to name a special prayer. When all have been given an opportunity to do so, the presider addresses all the sick:

Presider: You have each named a special prayer of your own,
and have heard each other's special prayers.
Will you pray for each other
that God may bless you all?

Some word or gesture of assent is invited, for example:

The Sick: We will.

The presider then addresses all who are gathered:

Presider: And you who gather in love
with this blessed community of faith and hope,
will you join in prayer for all the sick
that God will heal them and give them peace?

All: We will.

OPENING PRAYER

Presider   Then let us now pray:

Good and gracious God,
in your Son Jesus Christ,
you reach out to the sick
and touch them with your healing power.

Be with us now with this same healing power.

You hear the desires of our brothers and sisters
who come before you in hope and in trust.
You see us all
gathered in love before you.

Show yourself once more
a God who blesses and cares and gives peace.
We ask this through Christ our Lord.

All: Amen.

Liturgy of the Word

Presider: And now let us listen and take comfort
in the word God speaks to us.

READING: Isa 43:1-4a.

RESPONSORIAL PSALM: Ps 63

℞. My soul is thirsting for you, O Lord my God.

GOSPEL ACCLAMATION: cf. Jas 1:12

Alleluia.
Blessed are they who stand firm when trials come;
when they have stood the test,
they will win the crown of life.
Alleluia.

GOSPEL: Matt 11:25-30

Other appropriate readings, psalms and verses may be chosen from among those offered in *Pastoral Care of the Sick*, Part III.

HOMILY

See essay above (p. 90) for a pastoral description of the content and style required by a homily in this setting.

INTERCESSIONS

These may be composed by the presider or by some other minister, or they may be taken from *Pastoral Care of the Sick* #122, 138.

Liturgy of Anointing

INSTRUCTION

Presider: My brothers and sisters,
we come now to the time of special grace,
the time of anointing.

The apostle James asked:
"Are there people sick among you?
Let them send for the priests of the Church,
and let the priests pray over them,
anointing them with oil in the name of the Lord.
The prayer of faith will save the sick
and the Lord will raise them up.
if they have committed any sins,
their sins will be forgiven them."

My brothers and sisters
who are sick among us,
it is our privilege as a priestly people
to pray God's healing and anointing upon you.

Know that it is in your power
to offer even your sickness
as a gift of worship to God.

In God's power may you be healed.

LAYING ON OF HANDS

Joined by some of the friends and family, the presider goes to the sick one by one, places hands on each of them, and prays silently.

ANOINTING

The presider then anoints the sick on the forehead and hands, saying:

(anointing the forehead)

Through this holy anointing
may the Lord in his love and mercy help you
with the grace of the Holy Spirit.

All: Amen.

(anointing the hands)

> May the Lord who frees you from sin
> save you and raise you up.

All: Amen.

> (*Pastoral Care of the Sick #124, 141*)

PRAYER AFTER ANOINTING

When all have been anointed, the presider invites the sick to join hands, if this is possible, during the following prayer:

Presider: Good and gracious God,
God of love, ever-caring,
we give you praise and thanks
through your Son, Jesus Christ.

In him you show us how much you love us.
In him you have tasted
the beauty and the pain of all human life.

Those who were sick came to him
and found healing.
Those who had sinned asked of him
and found your forgiveness.

With oil that is blessed
and hearts that are humbled
we have anointed our sisters and brothers
here present.

With us at their side
they offer to you
their fears and their doubts,
their suffering and pain,
their human lives, fragile and broken.

Send your own Spirit of love upon them.
Speak the healing words of your Son to them.
Give them the grace of your loving presence.

Keep their eyes fixed firmly upon you
in the eager hope and expectation
that with you, and with you alone,
their lives will be transformed.

Where sin and death will be no more,
where sickness and sorrow will be overcome,

there may we know together
that you are our God,
and we the people you call your own.

All glory be to you, Father,
and to your Son,
and to your Holy Spirit,
now and forever.

All: Amen.

If this service of anointing takes place apart from the Eucharist, the
Lord's Prayer and a final blessing follow.

If it takes place during the celebration of the Eucharist, the liturgy
continues as usual:

Liturgy of the Eucharist

If possible, while the gifts are brought to the altar, some personal
effect of each of the sick is also to be brought forward. This serves
to unite their own sickness and suffering symbolically with the offering of Christ enacted in the Eucharist.

At the sign of peace, where it is possible, the sick extend the greeting to each other.

The following orations are suggested:

PRAYER OVER THE GIFTS

Presider: Lord our God, giver of all good gifts,
from among the many you have given to us
we bring bread and wine to give you thanks and
        praise.

In simple gifts we bring all that we are
and all that we hope for.

Look with special kindness
on our brothers and sisters who are sick among us.
Give them healing and peace.

Be pleased with us and the offering of our lives.
Unite us to Christ
and his own sacrifice of praise.

We ask this through Christ, our Lord.

All: Amen.

CONCLUDING PRAYER

Presider: Lord Jesus Christ,
you are the beginning and the end
of all God's creation.

You have gone before us to prepare the way.
Yet you remain among us as companion and friend.

As you have nourished us with your own food of life,
help us to be strong in faith,
a source of courage to each other,
and a gift of praise
to the God you have revealed.

We ask this in your name,
for you live and reign forever and ever.

All: Amen.

PASTORAL NOTE

There will, of course, be some who will not be able to participate in this communal form of anointing. For the long-term ill, the
regular enactment of this anointing will serve as the *context*, the
"world remembered," when they no longer can participate with the
others. For these, it would be helpful if some of the "community
of the sick" join in the prayer of the anointing. For others too it
would be helpful if some continuity with this communal celebration could be established so that the witness it represents may be
a ministry to all who are anointed in whatever circumstances it
proves necessary to anoint them. It might be helpful to conclude
the communal service with a "dismissal" that sends those who have
been anointed to minister in some way to those who were not able
to attend. The anointing of these others would then be held as part
of the communal celebration itself.

ALTERNATIVE 2: RITUALS OF HEALING FOR FAMILIES OF THE TERMINALLY ILL

Mary Frances Duffy, G.N.S.H.

Introduction

From its earliest times, the Christian community has addressed itself to God in prayer on behalf of the sick and the dying (Jas 5:13-16). Although in more recent times this sacramental act had found itself restricted to those who were *in extremis*, the post-Vatican II Church has once again expanded the scope of its sacramental pastoral care. In the restored rite of anointing, the Church's concern reaches out to all who are sick, even where the illness does not necessarily lead them to the doorway of death. In addition, recognizing that a single illness can last a long time and can be served by such prayer on more than one occasion, the Church allows the anointing to be repeated within an illness over a period of time.

Nevertheless, the focus of the sacrament has been and remains the sick and the dying. The action of the Church has not directly addressed those who attend the sick and the dying, those, that is, who are tied in relationship to the sick person by love and blood and/or by professional service and ministry. In current practice, if the people surrounding the sick person are to receive any comfort or consolation from the prayer of anointing, it will have to be indirectly and vicariously derived. To the extent that the patient is strengthened, consoled, granted peace, or even restored to health, to that extent alone can the sacrament be said to be efficacious in a derivative way for those who are close to the patient.

In an effort to address this pastoral gap, the rituals presented here are offered to minister to the unique emotional and spiritual needs of those persons who are affected by the illness of someone they love. Their particular focus is the family, friends, and caregivers who surround the terminally ill because their experience of impending loss is the more apparent. However, both the principles and the rituals which follow can be realistically applied or adapted to those confronted with the implicit loss which, as Jennifer Glen notes, is the consequence of every experience of serious illness, whether it be terminal or not. These rituals provide the Christian community with an opportunity to engage in a ministry of presence and support, perhaps simply "being there" to a group of people who are all too often left standing alone, keeping solitary vigil at home, in hospitals, or in nursing homes. Even more, and beyond the ministry of *compassionate presence* which these rituals attempt to offer, there is a ministry of *hospitality* which welcomes a group of alienated, marginalized persons of sorrow. There is also a ministry of *hope* which can help to extend the gaze of tear-filled eyes beyond the darkness of sickness and even of death to the lightsome promise of newness of life.

In their behavioral science and theological essays, Orlo Strunk and Jennifer Glen identify the relational character of sickness and death. Using the language of systems, Strunk speaks of the need for pastoral care "to widen its vision to include the families as well as the 'identified patient.'" He offers insight into the possibility of healing which may extend far beyond the realm of physical cure into the lives of persons other than a single terminally ill patient. Similarly, Glen has elaborated the social dimensions of sickness and death, the relational fabric of human life, and the communal character of liturgical ritual. Each, following the path marked out by his/her proper discipline, points to the same conclusion, namely, that there is need for liturgical ritual to gather explicitly those who intimately co-suffer with a dying person into the embrace of its prayer. This alternative future for worship attempts to respond to that need.

Those who attend to the sick and keep vigil with the dying need to know that they do not do so alone. Theirs is often a long loneliness in which there are few, if any, willing to offer presence, hospitality, and hope, and thus make the weeks and months of watchful waiting bearable, and perhaps even life-giving. It is little wonder that those who are signed with the cross of anticipatory mourning while awaiting the arrival of death are relegated to the darkened corridors and empty waiting rooms of sterile and medically proficient health-care institutions. In our death-denying society few people are genuinely able to cope with post-mortem grief, much less handle bereavement before death has happened. Ignored as shadows in the shadows, the family and friends of the terminally ill are left to deal with their emotional and psychological upheaval alone, and on their own resources. In like manner, although the number of capable ministers is gradually increasing on the health-care scene, there are still too few to mediate the presence of "the God of all comfort and consolation who attends us in all our afflictions" (2 Cor 1:4) at a time when, in the agony of slow death, such a God is almost impossible to discover. Sensitive indeed must be the minister who ventures to speak a healing word at such a time.

The rituals presented here are an invitation along a path not previously taken in the course of the Church's officially sanctioned sacramental ministry. They invite the Church to be an authentic Christ-presence to people who are painfully and helplessly poised between the awesome mysteries of lingering life and gathering death. They are an affirmation of the Church's willingness to be "troubled further," as Jesus was, by those who mourn. This alternative future for worship is offered as a profession of belief and trust that the Christian community can and will be the incarnate presence of the compassionate Christ engendering faith and offering hope, sharing grief and loss, speaking comfort and consolation, and touching the hands and hearts of those who die with the dying and who need themselves to hear and see and feel the Master's gentle command, "Do not be afraid; only have faith" (Mark 5:36).

These are rituals for a very particular group of persons. This specific group constitutes a graced "community of sorrow" in our midst. These ritual alternative futures for worship are intended to be an experience of liturgical prayer with and for those who are most intimately involved with the terminally ill and dying persons. Indirectly, they are, of course, offered as prayer for the dying themselves. There is, however, a reversal of the direct and indirect intentionalities which have historically characterized the spirit and celebration of this sacrament.

These family members and friends, in their sorrow, *deserve* the healing touch of the compassionate Christ present in the sacrament of anointing. And Christ, who yearns to touch them, *deserves* a proper vehicle for that touch. To the family and friends of the sick and the dying, the Church may well offer the sacramental ministry of healing through anointing even as Jesus extended himself beyond the dead and dying in service to those who mourn.

BIBLICAL BASIS FOR THE RITUAL

There is certainly biblical warrant for this proposal. In the midst of an impressive number and variety of miracle stories in which Jesus restores men and women to health and wholeness, there are several of particular significance to our consideration. These accounts provide a biblical rationale for an appropriate celebration of the sacrament with those who are themselves neither sick nor dying but are instead intimately associated with terminally ill patients.

On several occasions, Jesus is presented by an evangelist as being concerned about and involved with not only those who are suffering from illness and handicap but also with persons who have died or are dying. In more than one situation, what is even more striking is the care and compassion of Jesus evidenced toward the family and friends of the dead or dying individual. Jesus reveals himself to be a man of deep feeling. He recognizes their sorrow, sympathizes with their grief, and touches their pain, intimately and directly. In every situation of healing and restoration, Jesus offers the ultimate empathic response.

It is not difficult to imagine the emotional upheaval and psychological confusion raging within the heart and spirit of each scriptural character as he or she grapples with the devastating reality of death's separation and finality. Who among us has not known that same internal chaos?

In Mark 5 the evangelist presents Jesus confronted with a grieving parent as Jairus pleads earnestly for him to come and lay hands upon his daughter and save her life. There is little, if any, grief more intense than that of a parent for a lost child. Obediently, Jesus goes with him. While on the way it is learned that the little girl is already dead. To the grief-stricken father Jesus speaks words of comfort: "Do not be afraid; only have faith" (5:36).

Faith's reward is that of a twelve-year-old girl restored to life and given something to eat at the command of the Master. He allows himself to be "troubled further" by a bereaved parent and also by the very ordinary, mundane need of human beings to receive nourishment.

In Luke 7 we read the account of a centurion's servant "sick and

near death." The servant is restored to health by Jesus. The point
of interest and focus of concern in this accounting is not primarily
the servant healed of his illness. Rather, it is the Roman official who
experiences anticipatory grief over the impending loss of a favorite
servant and who, according to the Jewish elders, is deserving of
Jesus' favor. Encountering the centurion, Jesus is greeted with an
expression of humble belief so profound that he declares its like is
not to be found, even in Israel. Once again, in the face of death,
faith triumphs over grief. The belief of one, intensified and purified in the crucible of sorrow, proves efficacious for the life of
another.

The deep compassion of Jesus for those who mourn is presented
again in Luke 7. Jesus and his companions "happen" upon a funeral
procession. Ultimately, it turns out to be quite a happening! In what
is possibly one of the most tender and poignant sentences in the
Gospel narratives, we learn that Jesus "felt sorry" for the widow
of Nain who had lost her only son in death. Addressing the woman
in simple, direct language, Jesus tells her: "Do not cry" (7:13). Sensitive to the woman's lonely condition of widowhood, now intensified by the death of her only child, Jesus offers a response of
compassionate action. Touching the bier, he commands the man
"to get up." Having restored him to life, Jesus "return(s) him to his
mother." What joy she must have known! In all the world is there
any more precious gift than to receive again into our hand the life
of a loved one snatched from the grip of death?

A still more powerful display of Jesus' compassion toward those
who mourn the loss of a loved one may be found in John 11. Very
deliberately John tells of Jesus' deep emotional response upon learning of the death of his friend Lazarus. Beyond an experience of personal grief, Jesus is moved by the tears of Mary and the friends
who accompany her. Jesus inquires "in great distress, with a sigh
that came straight from the heart, 'Where have you put him?'"
(11:34). Upon seeing the place, we are told that "Jesus wept." With
those few words the evangelist confirms our belief, satisfies our desire, rewards our hope, and fulfills our need to know that Jesus himself experienced bereavement. Assurance is also given that Jesus was
touched deeply by the grief of those whom he loved as friends.

Additional confirmation of the concern for others in times of
sorrow, confusion, and faltering faith which elicits Jesus' empathy
is discovered in the prayer John places in the heart and upon the
lips of Jesus immediately prior to calling Lazarus forth from the

grave: ". . . but I speak for the sake of all these who stand around me, so that they may believe it was you who sent me" (11:42).

As in two of the previously cited episodes which reveal the depth and intensity of Jesus' feeling for those who mourn, again there is reference to the importance and necessity of believing.

At a time when one's total self is rent asunder, when physical, emotional, psychological, and spiritual energies are most severely strained, when depression, desperation, and despair threaten to gain overwhelming control, *then* it is that faith can mend the wrenching tear, restore depleted strength, and conquer the powers of darkness. At a time when the pain of loss and separation plunges one profoundly into the crucible of suffering and pierces so deeply that the wound appears beyond healing and the crucible beyond redemptive escape, when regret, remorse, and guilt become intimate companions of grief, when death for oneself seems a welcome relief, *then* it is that a person of faith is called to an experience and exercise of believing beyond what seems humanly possible.

The quality of faith demanded at such a time is not, cannot, and will not be experienced or exercised in isolation. Nor did Jesus give any indication or hint that such was his expectation or intention for those who mourn. Rather, for the grieving persons whose lives intertwined with his and whose grief moves him to compassionate, responsive action, faith was commanded *in* his physical presence, even *by* his physical presence. The grieving men and women of Scripture could see pain and sorrow in his eyes, hear grief and empathy in his voice, and touch and be touched by his strong yet gentle body and gather strength from his presence among them. Hopefully, it is neither too simplistic nor too presumptuous to suggest that whatever the difficulties to be overcome, their faithing was made easier by the Master's simply being there in a time of intense sorrowful need. For them, God's Word was flesh and blood —living, loving, weeping, and mourning—among them. Beyond offering comfort and consolation by his presence, he engendered hope in Someone and something beyond himself. Toward this reality he directed the eyes and hearts of those called to believe.

At this juncture, a question is raised: "What has all that to do with the anointing of the sick?" Without a moment's hesitation, the answer is an unequivocal: "Everything!"

PSYCHOLOGICAL BASIS FOR THE RITUAL

Persons responsible for the creation of ritual enactments in a parish or health-care setting will do well to remember several important considerations which influence the design and celebration of ritual prayer. The first is that rituals ideally arise from within the context of a broader and more comprehensive lived experience, the scope of which extends far beyond the fragile boundaries of the ritual itself. Ritual should never appear to come "from outer space"; rather, meaningful ritual expresses symbolically an all-embracing care and concern offered by the community of faith to those who mourn. Ritual is most true when woven into the total fabric of pastoral ministry to the dying and grieving in our midst.

A second consideration is the need to address the present moment in the unfolding drama of life and death. Dying and grieving persons are suspended uniquely between birth and death. They are in process, in evolution, in a liminal experience of time and space which is acutely painful. Rituals which attempt to address this experience must do exactly that: address the experience of grief and death. Sacramental ministry to the dying and grieving must recognize and reverence the emotional, spiritual, and psychological depth of the moment. Too often rituals for the dying and/or grieving turn a blind eye and deaf ear to the painful emotions of the present. Mourners are thrust prematurely into the hope-filled future. Compassionate pastoral care, including liturgy, leads mourners gently into the future through the present. Such ministry provides a therapeutic dimension which facilitates the catharsis of pain and an eschatological aspect which fosters hope.

The ritual design and content of these alternative celebrations has been inspired by the five-stage process of death and dying identified by Swiss psychiatrist Elisabeth Kübler-Ross, to whom members of the helping professions, including religion, owe a deep debt of gratitude. Although her work has already been noted above by Strunk, a brief treatment is included here as well because of the relationship between her stage theory and the rituals which follow.

Kübler-Ross' work is empirically based. Working with a group of graduate students at the University of Chicago's Billings Hospital, she interviewed a representative variety of terminally ill patients and their families. From these conversations, she identified what have come to be known as the five stages of death and dying. Comprising a dynamic process, these five stages are the basis for these alternative rituals of anointing. Kübler-Ross' research reveals that the stages are experienced not only by the terminally ill patients themselves, but also by their families and friends, and even by the medical personnel in attendance. She maintains:

We cannot help the terminally ill patient in a really meaningful way if we do not include his/her family. They play a significant role during the time of illness and their reactions will contribute a lot to the patient's response to his/her illness.[1]

The family too must be aided.

A brief description of each stage will facilitate an understanding of the ritual proposed. These descriptions are suggestive rather than exhaustive:

Stage 1: Denial and Isolation[2]

"Not me! This can't be happening to me. It is a mistake."

The person searches for hope; may consult a new doctor, and seek a new diagnosis; becomes withdrawn and aloof. Denial has a variety of attitudinal and behavioral manifestations.

Stage 2: Anger[3]

"Why me?"

The person experiences rage at the injustice of death and fear of being forgotten. Anger may be communicated verbally and/or nonverbally. Anger may be directed toward family, friends, medical staff, or God. Behavior is often misunderstood and difficult to deal with for persons who are the object of displaced anger.

Stage 3: Bargaining[4]

"If I am good, can I gain more time?"

The person makes deals and promises; becomes cooperative; sets short or long-range goals. As each is met, other goals are established, e.g., "If I can just live to see my son married" or ". . . until Christmas" or ". . . until springtime." The sufferer gambles with time, fate, doctors, God.

Stage 4: Depression[5]

There is reactive depression, e.g., at loss of health or job or to the monetary cost of illness.

There is also preparatory depression at loss of life itself and of loved ones.

Stage 5: Acceptance[6]

"I'm ready now."

The person accepts the inevitability of death. It is a time of peace. This stage requires enough time in order to occur and necessitates people to assist in the process rather than to conflict with the "letting go." This stage may seem to family and friends to be a rejection of them as acceptance is embraced and love relationships are peacefully relinquished.

Critics of the Kübler-Ross research suggest that the stages do not go far enough. Religious critics especially contend that the process fails to recognize a stage of joyful expectation or anticipation characteristic of the Christian understanding of life after death, with its resulting full and final communion with God. To a degree this criticism is correct. It must be understood, however, that Kübler-Ross approached the phenomenon of death from the psychological perspective of her particular discipline. It is from that vantage point that she has spoken. Perhaps it is the task of Christian believers, especially persons engaged in ministry to the dying and grief-stricken, to assume the responsibility appropriate to their professions concerning the theological and spiritual ramifications of this process. And certainly there are such ramifications. Their discovery, exploration, and integration will help all Christians extend their understanding of the death process and will invite them to enter more deeply into the vast, uncharted regions of both the human spirit and their own Christian faith.

Religion and psychology can and must work together in the arena of pastoral care. They can help each other reverently probe the mystery of sickness and death, and together come to utter a fuller word of life, hope, and joyous anticipation. Where this is done, where men and women show themselves of sufficient compassion and courage to enter and speak from within the sacred space that belongs to the sick and the dying in a manner similar to that of Elisabeth Kübler-Ross, such will be a service well rendered.

Personal Background to the Ritual

Both the concern which gave rise to the rituals to come and the rituals themselves are rooted in a personal grappling with the phenomenon of death and dying as it strikes the family and friends of the sick. How do the healthy deal with sickness when it strikes someone they love?

For me, the journey began almost twelve years ago. As an instructor in religious education in a Catholic secondary school, I was asked to assume responsibility for teaching a course entitled "On Death and Dying," which was new to the curriculum.

The program of study challenged me on levels I had not anticipated. While I had delighted to teach young adults about life and living, I found myself much less comfortable when the issue turned to death and dying. I felt inauthentic and dishonest in my attempts to provide answers and assuage fears. In the process of preparation and presentation, I was discovering the depth and breadth of my own unresolved questions and anxieties.

The course itself proved somewhat of a conversion experience. I found I could not be a teacher from strength, but rather had to become with my students a fellow student and questioner, unafraid of my own doubts and uncertainties. As student, I learned. It is as student I write.

The subsequent journey has brought me into the life and death stories of countless men and women, young and old, with whom I have shared privileged and sacred moments as we have explored the meaning of living and dying. They have come from every station and walk of life, from every religious tradition and political persuasion. Among them have been the terminally ill, the grieving, the weak and the strong, those still fresh along life's journey, and those well on their way to their own passage through death. Yet all shared a common quest: for insight, understanding, and hope.

The most fundamental link of bondedness was, of course, a shared humanity which recognized, often in vague and inarticulate ways, a common destiny. Each would some day have to confront and contend with the reality of their own sickness and death. That recognition gave rise to a search which may be called by many names: for meaning, for a reason, for a way to cope, for a way to prepare, for an anchor to hold on to, for something in which to believe and hope.

Even more important than the name of the search were the affective qualities which characterized it: feelings of loss, of pain, of fear; feelings of anger, of alienation and of loneliness; feelings of intense negativity. But a more remarkable revelation of our journeys together was the subtle, yet clear and powerful beam of light which was somehow generated in the midst of darkness and its negatives. The *koinonia* of believers together gave birth to hope and light and release from the bondage that the negatives produced.

It is this gentle voice of life which these rituals for the healthy in the face of sickness and death hope to serve. Anger and confusion, fear and loneliness, loss and pain, all these will invariably play themselves out in those who must stand by powerless as someone they love succumbs to sickness and the journey into death. These cannot be avoided; they must have their say. At the same time there is another voice which must be heard, a voice of healing, of hospitality, of hope. It is a voice needed by the healthy as well as the sick.

The Ritual

Before presenting a sample structure for an alternative ritual, it seems appropriate to offer some suggestions on how the rituals are to be enacted, including considerations of setting, environment, size, tone and length of the rite.

Settings. There are several possible settings for a ritual of this type. They include but are not limited to the parish, the hospital, and the home.

Parish Setting: Staff members associated with the parish health-care ministry will most probably be familiar with the persons for whom and with whom these rituals might be celebrated. Such persons could be invited to participate in a celebration of the sacrament offered only for people confronted with the terminal illness of a loved one. They in turn might be encouraged to invite friends and associates.

Another alternative is to announce the celebration of the sacrament to the entire parish community so that as many persons as possible might be present in prayerful support of those facing the loss of a loved one. This would also allow for participation by persons whose own personal grief may not be generally known. As in the first instance, persons associated with dying patients might be given a more personal invitation to attend.

The ministers in the community ought to be especially mindful of the needs and sensitivities of those for whom the anointing is being offered. It may happen that some will refuse the invitation. This should not be interpreted negatively, as, for example, lack of gratitude or weakness of faith. More likely it will be indicative of the style or stage of coping operative in the grieving persons. In such cases, other pastoral alternatives might be required.

Hospital Setting: Parish ministers assigned to health care chaplaincy or pastoral-care personnel might arrange for a celebration of the sacrament for the families and friends of the sick in the hospital chapel or some other appropriate place. Again, participation could be encouraged either by personal invitation or by general announcement. In hospitals and other health-care environments such as nursing homes, doctors and nurses could likewise be invited to participate. In some situations it might be appropriate to design a ritual for these helping professionals who must daily contend with the loss of patients through death.

Home Setting: In some circumstances it might be advantageous, even necessary, to provide for the celebration of the sacrament in a more private setting. The pastoral awareness and sensitivities of the health-care minister concerning some patients and their families might indicate a need for a personal, intimate ceremony on familiar home territory. The parish or hospital minister might have to suggest such a celebration rather than wait for the family or friends to request it.

Environment. The specific space designated for the ceremony should be as comfortable and aesthetically pleasing as possible. Creating attitude and atmosphere is essential. Quiet music, soft lighting, tasteful artifacts such as candles, plants, flowers, vessels, and table coverings, all contribute their beauty to the graceful celebration of the rite. In the face of sickness and death, the total celebration of the ritual—word, silence, gesture, and environment—must unite in offering healing, hospitality and hope to participants.

Size. It is probably safe to assume that most celebrations of this ritual would be small. Thus it is possible, and even desirable, to foster a certain level of informality. Compassion, gentility, and warmth are important qualities. Informal though it may be, however, it is never intended that the ritual be casual. Care must be exercised to ensure a delicate balance.

Tone. A contemplative tonality is important to the ritual enactment. Creating a "space before God" in which the participants can simply "be with" God, themselves, their emotions, and one another is best served by a contemplative atmosphere. A gentle, alternating rhythm between sound and silence is to be encouraged.

Length. If for no other reason than the physical and emotional fatigue associated with grief, the length of the service should be approximately one-half hour. Celebrations for larger groups may require additional time. However, care should be taken to avoid taxing the already strained energies of the participants.

The following ritual sample is intended to be *both* a single celebration of the sacrament of anointing for family and friends of those who are sick *and* a ritual structure that may be adapted according to the Kübler-Ross stages of death and dying. For this reason, an appendix to the full ritual offers alternative texts for the instruction and Scripture reading to be used at each stage.

Introductory Rites

GATHERING

The presider and other participating ministers greet the assembly at the entrance to the worship space to extend an initial sense of hospitality and welcome. When all are assembled, the ministers enter in procession, accompanied by instrumental music.

CALL TO WORSHIP AND GREETING

Presider: My brothers and sisters:

In the name of our Lord Jesus Christ I welcome you.
I invite you to come to him who says
to the weary, the burdened, and the sorrowing:
"Come to me and I will give you rest."

Place yourselves now in Christ's compassionate
    presence.
He desires to share your pain
so that he may sorrow with you
and grant you peace.

May the Lord be with you.

All: And also with you.

OPENING SONG

OPENING PRAYER

Presider: Let us pray.

God of all comfort and consolation,
be with us now in our prayer.
We suffer with those who suffer;
we die with those who die.

Touch us in the deepest recesses of our grief,
in those hidden places we fear to acknowledge
or give to your keeping.

Help us be compassionate
toward those who are sick.
Help us be gentle with ourselves.

May we come to understand and accept
the mystery of sickness and death
which holds our loved one(s) in its grip.

In the fullness of time and in the slowness of our
    hearts
speak to us your word of comfort and your word of
    peace.

We ask this in the power of the Spirit
and in your Son, Jesus Christ, the Lord.

All: Amen.

INSTRUCTION

Presider: The journey of life brings each of us, at one time or another, to a place of pain. Without our will we are brought into life; against our will we are forced to confront the pain of sickness and the sorrow of death.

Each of you knows the pain associated with the sickness and death of those you love. Your concern is for them, and yet your own hearts are torn apart. Your own lives are disrupted.

This pain and disruption you may nobly try to deny; yet it is there. It may bring you anger, or lead you to bargain with God and with life "if only things could be different." Or it may make you very, very sad.

Yet, however you feel at this moment, the healing power of Christ seeks to touch your hearts. He seeks to lead you to accept and embrace this life with all its mystery, and to discover his love for you in the midst of this sadness and grief.

May we spend a few moments in quiet reflection before our God, and allow ourselves to experience honestly and with reverence the feelings which are uniquely our own. Let us express ourselves to God in truth, without fear or shame.

REFLECTIVE SILENCE

Liturgy of the Word

READING: Matt 26:36-46

HOMILY

The homily is usually given by the presider or by some other person invited to provide this ministry. In some situations, however, it may be appropriate to invite the participants to share their reflections on the scripture reading in the format of a dialogue homily.

PSALM/SONG OF HOPE AND TRUST

At the end of the homily, some form of common prayer or song is appropriate as both a conclusion to the Word and a transition into prayers of petition.

PRAYER OF PETITION

Presider: My brothers and sisters,
the God to whom Jesus prayed for deliverance
invites each of us to be healed.
In Jesus we find the hope that makes us whole
and the promise that life is forever.

God is no stranger to our human pain and suffering.
In Jesus God has embraced our own human life
even to the point of suffering and death.
In Jesus God has become companion to us
in our own journey through life.
"Behold, I am with you all days";
"I make my abode with you."

Unite then your sorrow to the dying and rising of Christ.
Believe and your faith will make you whole.
In faith and in hope be companion to those
with whom you keep vigil,
your loved ones for whom we now pray:

All in the assembly are invited to pray in their own words for their loved ones and for themselves. If it is helpful the presider may form the first several petitions. After the petitions:

Presider: Loving God,
Lord of all health and wholeness,
you are source of our life
and fulfilment of our death.

We come to you now with varied needs.
Into your gentle care we place ourselves
and our loved ones who are ill.

Be for us now
light to brighten our darkness,
strength to transform our weakness,
and comfort in the midst of our pain.

> We ask this in the power of the Spirit
> through Christ, our Lord.

All: Amen.

Rite of Anointing

ANOINTING

Presider: My brothers and sisters,
as a sign of our faith
and in hope for the healing embrace of God,
come forward now
to be anointed with holy oil.

May Jesus Christ
who is infinite compassion
touch you and bless you,
and give you his healing grace.

As each member of the assembly comes forward, he/she is anointed on both forehead and hands. The presider prays the accompanying prayer:

Presider:

(anointing the head)

> May God heal your own wounds
> as you stand in hope
> with N. who is ill.

(anointing the hands)

> May God give you
> eyes to see and ears to hear
> and hands that you may touch
> and bless and understand.[7]

When all have received the sacrament of the anointing, there follows a brief period of silence.

COMMON PRAYER: Ps 23

The service concludes with Ps 23 recited or sung in common. If desired, the Lord's Prayer or a suitable prayer of praise and thanksgiving may be prayed instead.

Concluding Rites

DISMISSAL

Presider: Signed with the cross of Christ,
and touched with his healing grace,
go forth now from this place
to serve God's people
in compassion, kindness, and love.

All: Thanks be to God.

CLOSING SONG

Appendix: Alternative Texts for the Stages of Death and Dying

The suggestions that follow are intended to serve in the adaptation of the above ritual to the various stages of death and dying as cited above. Both instruction and Scripture text are to be inserted within the above ritual in their designated places.

Alternative for Stage 1: Denial

INSTRUCTION

The human confrontation with sickness and death almost always meets with some form of denial, at least in its initial stages. We seek to pretend it away. "It can't be happening; it can't be true." This is true for those who fall sick. It is equally true of those who love them.

Our prayer today invites you to look squarely at your own deep reactions to the sickness that has come upon people you love. It may be hard to believe it is happening to them. But since their own sickness reveals how deeply your lives are connected to theirs, you may find it equally hard to believe it is happening to you.

To deny sickness in those who are sick is a refusal to accept them as they now are. And this at a time when they most need to be accepted. To hide your own fears and denial behind well intended words that promise "all will be well" is in fact a denial of truth and a rejection of those whom you love.

Now more than ever they need you to be true. Now more than ever you need to be true. Both they and you need to speak in truth for only in truth will faith be able to speak, hope be able to serve, and love be able to deepen.

Christ does not hide from the deepest truth of our lives. He loves us when we sin; he embraces us when we are sick.

Let us spend a few moments in quiet reflection before Jesus Christ and let the truth of what is happening to our loved ones and to ourselves come deeply into our hearts. And let him who is Truth itself comfort us and bring us deep peace.

READING: Matt 16:21-23

Peter denies Jesus' impending suffering and death.

Alternative for Stage 2: Anger

INSTRUCTION

On days when all is well, it is easy to be happy with God. It is also easy to ignore God, or simply to take God for granted. When all is not well, when sickness strikes us or someone we love, we are much more likely to feel betrayed by God and to become very angry.

And our anger goes not only to God but in so many directions. To the one who is sick: "Why are you doing this to me?" To the doctors and givers of care: "Why can't you do more?" To others in the family: "Why don't you do your share?" And to just about anyone else who may happen to come our way.

Jesus himself was angry in the face of his death. At Judas, who was impatient to betray him. At Philip, who was slow to understand, and at Peter whose pretended bravery was but a form of denial. And he was angry at God, his Father, who demanded much and yet seemed to abandon him.

If anger fills your hearts this day, place it with him who has known anger and yet passed beyond its grip. Place it with him who quiets all anger and fear with a glance, a touch, a silent word.

READING: John 18:10-11

Simon Peter, angry at Jesus' arrest, draws a sword.

Alternative for Stage 3: Bargaining

INSTRUCTION

There is a game we play in the face of sickness and death, perhaps as a retreat into denial or a defense against anger. We bargain with God, with life, with ourselves.

We bargain with the past, and fill ourselves with false regrets that we should have done what we did not do. "If only I had . . . ," the bargain goes.

And we bargain with the future, making all sorts of promises, equally false, of what we will do if only . . . .

The irony is that we waste the time that is ours looking for time that is not ours and will not be. And the precious time that is ours, to speak and to care and to love, quickly passes us by.

This time is given to each of us, not to pass it in idle wish or vain desire, but rather
—to speak, as perhaps we have not spoken before;
—to care, as perhaps we have not cared before;
—to love, as perhaps we have not loved before;
—and to believe deeply and to trust in the ways of God.

This time is given to those you love. This time is given to you. Take it and use it well.

READING: Luke 22:41-46

Jesus prays for the cup of suffering to pass.

Alternative for Stage 4: Depression

INSTRUCTION

The passage of sickness can be long and tedious, wearing away at all resources to cope, bear with, endure. A vigil with those who are sick can likewise be long and tedious, and likewise wear away one's own personal resources. In the end we can grow very tired of it all, and simply sad.

Such sadness or depression can leave us locked in our own world, a world that has grown smaller as all avenues of escape seem to close. It is hard to minister to those who are depressed. It is hard to minister when we ourselves are without hope.

In your own vigil with your loved one(s) no doubt your energies have been spent. Well spent, yet spent. And if you are sad, it is a sadness you need to understand if you will help someone else to pierce its deep dark mystery.

You will seem to be surrounded by silence. Yet deeper than silence, and within the silence itself, there waits a word to be heard. A word of courage and a word of hope.

In the silence of your hearts listen now to the whispers that alone will redeem the sadness. Let the Lord who has gone before us all speak gently, yet powerfully, where most you need him to speak.

READING: Matt 17:22-23

Jesus speaks of his coming suffering to his disciples.

Alternative for Stage 5: Acceptance

INSTRUCTION

In the garden, and again on the cross, Jesus gave his life and his sufferings over into the hands of his God. It was not a "giving in," nor even a "giving up." Jesus gave himself over to another who lovingly and graciously received his gift.

So often we are counselled to accept what is given to us. Perhaps from time to time we counsel others the same. But in that word we all too often forget the gift and the giving that acceptance involves. To see suffering, my suffering or the suffering of one I love, as a precious gift I can give in love to my God is the deepest secret of all human pain.

God is not far away from those who are sick, nor from those who keep vigil with the sick. God is present most deeply within the pain and the sorrow and the sadness, yearning to make of it all a gift of praise and glory. It takes deep faith and hope and love to give even pain as a gift to God. But such a gift reveals pain's deepest meaning and deepest possibility.

Look at your own pain and the pain of those you love, and listen. From deep within a voice may be heard; even now, "you are precious in my eyes, and honored, and I love you."

READING: Luke 23:44-46

Jesus commends his spirit to God.

Footnotes

1. Elisabeth Kübler-Ross, *On Death and Dying* (New York: Macmillan, 1969) 157.
2. *Ibid.* 38-49.
3. *Ibid.* 50-81.
4. *Ibid.* 82-84.
5. *Ibid.* 85-111.
6. *Ibid.* 112-137.
7. Adapted from J. L. L'Heureux, in *The Experimental Liturgy Book*, ed. R. Hoey (New York: Herder, 1969) 97.

ALTERNATIVE 3: A RITUAL OF HEALING FOR PERSONS IN MID-LIFE

Mary Frances Duffy, G.N.S.H.

Introduction

Recognizing the goodness of human life as created and redeemed by God, the Church offers sacramental companionship and ministry to believers throughout the course of a lifetime. Significant events, from birth to death, are rendered still more sacred through touching and being touched by the Holy in sacramental encounter.

As the behavioral sciences discover and reveal more of the dynamics operative in various stages of the human life cycle, as society becomes more complex, stressed and violent, as life expectancy is lengthened and the graying of America becomes increasingly evident, there will arise emotional, psychological and spiritual conditions of need which previously either did not exist or were not recognized. With the development and intensification of these conditions, the Church will be provided with the opportunity to extend the sacramental ministry of the compassionate Christ in new directions.

In approaching the task of creating alternative rituals of healing in contemporary American culture, I was guided by two questions: if Jesus Christ were visibly present in his historical person today, to whom would he offer his healing ministry? And whom would he wish the Church, as his living presence in the world, to touch and bless with the sacramental healing of anointing? Among the many answers which arose in response, I have chosen persons in mid-life for several reasons: because their name is Legion, because their psychological and spiritual stage of development is significant and influential in society and Church, and because I, numbered in their company, understand experientially the pitfalls and potentials, the problems and promises of their age.

In the opening behavioral science essay, Orlo Strunk identified "developmental principles" as one idiosyncratic factor which is all too often neglected in liturgical practice and yet which offers considerable promise for liturgical revision. Liturgical experience and liturgical need vary with the various ages and stages of life's journey. The experience of mid-life is an example *par excellence* of Strunk's observation. His reflections encourage me to put forward this ritual for persons in mid-life.

At the same time I recognize that the extension of the sacrament of anointing to persons in mid-life is not without problems. In her theological essay, Jennifer Glen raised a haunting and challenging question: "Are the Church's specifically designated rites of healing . . . equally appropriate for those whose lives have been disrupted by some other form of suffering?" It is a question for which there is no easy answer, but one which is quite to the point as I suggest the extension of this sacrament to persons whose life is indeed disrupted but by a suffering which is not necessarily physical in form.

I do share Glen's concern lest our liturgical rituals be stretched too thin, and thus become devoid of any specific meaning. I am equally concerned, however, that, much like a muscle atrophied by lack of exercise, our rituals may snap in our hands for not being stretched far enough. It is a fact that every experience of limit and loss brings with it the touch of death's bony finger, however subtly it be felt. Every experience of disruption and fragmentation brings with it a confrontation with one's fragility and mortality. Every experience of human limitation brings with it a threat to faith and hope and love and needs to be addressed in some fashion or other with the healing power of God in Christ.

My reason for suggesting this extension-by-analogy of the sacrament of anointing to persons in mid-life has more to do with "experiential content" that is, with the experience of human mortality and potential loss of ultimate meaning, than with the specific extrinsic causes which give rise to the experience, although the actual advance of life toward death is certainly a significant factor in that experience. Even if the passage of mid-life were not explicitly characterized by confrontations with finitude, bodily limitation, and human mortality, I would still advocate celebrating some form of the Church's healing sacrament for these people and for many others caught in the chaos and confusion of a collapsing meaning world. As it is, however, mid-life is in fact often enough so characterized and therefore rests more comfortably within Glen's theological framework. Her word of caution is well taken. But the risk, if there be one, is even more well taken.

In every experience of sacramental encounter which marks life's pilgrimage, the role of the Church is to serve as companion, guide, teacher, and support along the way. As the transformative process of mid-life leads ever onward and deeper into the mystery of transcendence, the dangers and obstacles confronted on the journey render the weary traveller vulnerable to detours and turnings back and away from pursuit of the ultimate destination. Thus the sacramental Church is rightly called upon to be a source of challenge, encouragement, and support which enables the pilgrim to remain faithful, patient, and persevering.

Mid-life wanderers need to remember again and again God's own faithfulness to them, which alone, in the words of Johannes Metz, will sustain their own fidelity.[1] It is the sacred privilege and awesome responsibility of the Church to provide, through the sacramental ministry of encounter with the compassionate Christ, an ever deepening and maturing experience of the faithful God in the course of life's transforming journey. That segment of the journey which passes through generativity to integration, through darkness to light, and through desert and dark wood to freedom during the mid-life transition deserves to be signed and sealed by the touch of God in the healing sacrament of anointing. Thus will the traveller be refreshed and strengthened and empowered to continue the journey.

MID-LIFE: THE EXPERIENCE

Recent years give evidence of a renewed or perhaps a new-found interest in adult development. Much of this interest focuses upon the growth which occurs during the middle and later stages of human life. The middle years have proven to be an ambivalent period in the life of the average adult. Some have indeed discovered that "life begins at forty." Others, not understanding the nature and meaning of the chaos and confusion suddenly unleashed within them at mid-life, have found themselves unable to negotiate creatively the turbulence threatening to engulf them. This ambivalence, felt by common people long before it was identified by the theorists, has prompted the study of every facet of the human person in an effort to unveil the mysterious phenomenon of mid-life experience. In order to appreciate the ritual which follows, it is necessary to have some understanding of the experience to which it is addressed as that experience has been explored and articulated by some of those theorists.

Given the fact that a sacramental rite brings faith to bear upon real life interpreted in light of the mystery of Jesus Christ, it is important to note that significant contributions have been and continue to be made to the quest for knowledge and understanding of mid-life by persons who concern themselves primarily with religion and the spiritual life. For men and women of faith, this is as it should be. The totality of human life from birth to death provides an arena for the inbreaking of the Holy and presents rich opportunity for a dialogic encounter of call and response between God and the creatures made in the divine image.

It is interesting to note that the language used to describe mid-life in both the religious and the non-religious literature finds deep resonance in the vocabulary of belief. Passage, journey, and transformation are a few of the now familiar symbols employed in reference to the mid-life experience. If such images carry deep significance for those who concern themselves primarily with the psychological and emotional aspects of mid-life, how much more meaningfully can they be applied to the same experience by those who approach human existence and all of its ages and stages from a spiritual perspective?

Certainly, for those who have eyes to see and ears to hear the hidden, whispering presence of God in all of life's experience, mid-life has the profound potential of becoming an exodus to freedom in radical conversion. Mid-life is a passage which carries one ever more deeply not only into the mystery of life but, more importantly, into the mystery of the Source of Life itself.

Closely related to the images of passage and journey used for spiritual growth and development are the symbols of desert and wilderness. The passage to freedom necessarily takes one through a barren, dry, and wasted land. Mid-life is such a terrain. The interior spaces feel as the psalmist graphically exclaims, "parched, lifeless and without water" (Ps 63:1) Between the ages of thirty-five and fifty-five, the storms which assail the spirit are capable of blinding the spiritual pilgrim caught in swirling clouds of dust and sand. The scorching heat of desire and longing alternates with the piercing chill of doubt and questioning. By day and by night, the mid-life desert is a frightening place in which to travel. Yet it is a desert which can burst forth in blossom.

In the deserts of mid-life, mirages beckon from every side and oases are few. As Gerard Connolly describes it:

> The way "inside" is a journey, a process, a way of being called out of "comfort" and slavery. As with Abraham or Moses with the Hebrews, the journey into the wilderness is unfamiliar, trackless. It is filled with resistances and temptations to idolatry as one's security is threatened.[2]

The temptation is to flee outward or at least to venture no further in. However, as with the physical reality of crossing the desert, so also with the symbolic passage through the wilderness of mid-life, the only way out is through. The conditions for survival are endurance and fidelity to the process of transformation. Sustained by the promise of the God of our nomadic ancestors, given also to us, the mid-life wanderer is challenged to remain faithful both to the promise itself and to the One who makes it.

The desert is one metaphor aptly applied to the transitions of mid-life. Dante's "dark wood" is another. Mid-life, often desolate, dry, and dusty, is also dark. It is, for many, a time devoid of illumination. Though the spirit's eye squints and strains to discern the path, the straight way ahead remains obscured. In the absence of light, one may stumble and fall or become ensnared in the tangles of emotional, psychological, and spiritual underbrush. There lurks the ever present danger of collision with obstacles not clearly perceived. More ominous still is the danger of becoming so lost as to abandon the search and to remain immobilized by fear and frustration, as deeply rooted in the darkness as the towering sentinels which populate the forest.

Whatever the images and symbols employed in descriptions of the mid-life transition, there are certain essential characteristics which mark and identify this period and process of adult development.

First, the crises of mid-life transition and transformation are not something which an individual chooses. Rather, the passage or "second journey"[3] which commences with the second half of life is something which happens to a person. Often it is precipitated by some external event which occurs unexpectedly and for which one is unprepared. A striking example is the second journey precipitated for Ignatius of Loyola by the wound he received at the battle of Pamplona. During a long period of recuperation, he reassessed the values and orientations of his life. Deciding to redirect his own course, he also changed the course of history.

In other instances the unrest and disorientation of the mid-life transition arise from within oneself. There is no clear external factor to explain the onset of doubt, fear, and questioning which one experiences. Without warning, one is set adrift on a turbulent sea of uncertainty and insecurity. Much, if not all, of what was once seen and held as valuable is now perceived as being without meaning. Power, position, prestige, success, and achievement, once so feverishly pursued, appear empty and foolish. One is haunted by the question, "Is that all there is?" but no satisfactory answers are forthcoming. Whether arising from within or from without, then, the storms of mid-life are not something for which one goes in search. Rather, the second journey is something which is thrust upon those who have lived long enough to find themselves in the dark wood.

Another almost invariable characteristic of the mid-life journey is that the internal movements of the experience have an external counterpart. Not infrequently, though the way is not clearly marked, there is relocation from one place to another. The internal promptings which motivate the search for new meanings suggest that these may be discovered in a new place with new activities and associates. The underlying affect upon which the quest is established is one of hope and a desire for new horizons. In a very real sense, travelling from one place to another in search of fresh beginnings is an exodus journey. Much of life, with its familiar patterns and pursuits, is recognized and rejected as "bondage in Egypt." Movement through the deserts and dark woods of mid-life offers the hope of freedom in a still-to-be-discovered "Promised Land."

The restlessness which characterizes the internal landscapes of mid-life often feels like the Exodus sojourn of forty years' wandering. And from a spiritual perspective, it is these internal feelings, movements, and dispositions that merit primary attention and concern. They can draw us closer to God and to ourselves; they can also alienate us from God and from ourselves. To cite Gerard Connolly once again:

> God communicates and draws us closer by making (his) presence known in the deepest movements of our hearts, e.g., insights, affective stirrings. In the same core area where this occurs we are also drawn away from God.[4]

The transition of mid-life is marked also by a significant crisis

of feelings. Affective equilibrium is set askew. During mid-life un-
negotiated developmental work from the past comes to the fore.
Psychosocial tasks from earlier ages and stages are reevaluated and
recapitulated. Unfinished business and unresolved conflicts from
younger days clamor for attention. Forgotten, neglected, and re-
pressed parts of the self proclaim their presence from within and
demand a hearing. Relationships with individuals and institutions
are subjected to intense scrutiny. Feelings, long denied or unrecognized, associated with these relationships, surge upward in a tor-
rent of chaos and confusion. Old questions resurface with heightened
meaning and intensity. One is confronted with having to ask yet
again: "Who am I? How do I love? Why do I love? Whom do I
love? What really matters? What is the meaning of my life? What
have I accomplished? What do I hope to accomplish in the time
that remains for me? Was/Is it all worth it? What do I want?" Such
questioning reveals that mid-life is a time of reassessment. It offers
the opportunity for taking stock of all that has been and for continuing or redirecting the course upon which one is set.

Of particular importance in the disturbance of feelings is a change
in one's sense of the reality of time—past, present, and future. There
is an urgency associated with the mid-life passage which originates
in a dawning realization of mortality. Life is not endless. Death
looms large on the horizon as an ever-present reminder that the dis-
tance from birth to the present moment may now be longer than
that which extends from the present to death. While thoughts of
death populate the mind, realizations of physical decline—fatigue,
loss of energy, wrinkles, somatic difficulties—unite in conspiracy
against any attempts to deny the unrelenting approach of old age
and death. Confronted with a life's road which is now viewed as
less long and winding, the time left in which to *be* and to do is treasured as more precious.

Physical decline and ultimate confrontation with the reality of
death thrusts a crisis of limits upon the mid-life pilgrim. One recognizes a sense of having to go where one would rather not be led.
In mid-life a person is forced to accept fragility and vulnerability,
restriction and limitation as never before. William Kraft writes:

> Many mid-life issues center around the experience of limits. As these
> enclose us they challenge us to seek deeper dimensions of life. In-
> stead of evoking depression, regression or escapism, the experience
> of limits is an opportunity to encounter the Unlimited. As the fini-
> tude of time calls forth the timeless, so the ultimate limit—death—
> renews life and generates the Infinite.[5]

Kraft reminds us that every new venture undertaken is rich with new possibilities. It may lead to new destinations or to a familiar destination viewed from a new perspective. And his naming of the Unlimited as the true horizon of the quest reminds us that here, at least as much as anywhere else in life, the full resources of one's religious faith are needed.

It is an inner quest. Much of the orientation toward external success and achievement typical of the earlier years is replaced by inclinations to go within. Interiority is the locus for the discovery of the "more" of life which was sought previously in external preoccupations. From the recesses of the interior depths there emerges a new and different sense of self—a self now more clearly defined by the realization that who one is is more important than what one does or what one has accomplished.

As the mid-life person travels through the desert and the dark wood, there is often a sense that one is very much alone and lonely.[6] It is not surprising during this time to discover feelings of alienation from those with whom one has been most involved and intimately associated. Alienation mingles with and intensifies feelings of loneliness. The mid-life experience of ultimate aloneness is a generous invitation to move beyond the wastelands of loneliness to the refreshing oasis of solitude. In befriending one's solitary condition there is a simultaneous embracing of a more authentically integrated self.

It may happen, of course, that the newly discovered meaning and sense of direction which eventually come with a successful negotiation of the mid-life pilgrimage will have a profound effect on the persons and groups from whom one felt separated. The results of the Ignatian mid-life transition are self-evident. In recent times Mother Teresa of Calcutta is a exemplary model of the impact which even one person, having passed through the dark wood, can exert upon an entire nation and even, the whole world.

Given the number of years chronologically associated with the passage of mid-life, it is evident that the full and final emergence into newness of life may take more than a few years of suffering and wrestling with demons of confusion, doubt, and fear. Possibly as at no other time in life, mid-life requires an heroic exercise of the virtues of faith, hope, and patience. This is particularly true because as with all processes of growth, the desired maturity and integration toward which mid-life journeying directs itself are achieved largely through patient, faith-filled waiting. Although the mid-life person is not totally passive in the process, beyond a certain point, efforts to hasten the passage prove futile. Just as one waits for the darkness of night to pass and the first faint glimmers of morning to penetrate and illumine the darkened silhouettes of the woodland, so too does one strain to glimpse even a tiny beam of light at the end of the mid-life tunnel.

In speaking of the end of the tunnel, O'Collins warns against the possibility of the journey ending in a less than creative, integrative manner.[7] Of particular significance are the possibilities of ending the journey prematurely or of choosing the wrong goal. In the first instance, patience wears thin. One simply abandons the search. As a result, a more integrated, stable, and mature way of life is sacrificed. The second instance reveals the danger of detours along the way which lead the mid-life traveller off-course and down a dead-end road to nothingness and nowhere. Truncation of the process admits that the pain is simply too great or the price is too costly to be paid. It is easier to settle for less than that to which life and the Source of Life invited and challenged.

MID-LIFE: THE PROMISE

Having identified briefly some of the essential characteristics of the mid-life process of growth toward integration, it is now appropriate to explore the nature of the call which is sounded from within the dark wood of mid-life. While the invitations of mid-life are many and varied, these explorations are here confined to three: conversion, compassion, and commitment. It is these three invitations which are reiterated and supported in the ritual which follows.

Even a superficial examination of the literature on mid-life and on conversion reveals that the same language is employed to describe the phenomenological content of both. In the unfolding of both processes, there is darkness, dryness, a sense of disoriented wandering through a desert. The onset of conversion, like that of mid-life, is not something which one is capable of effecting for oneself. Rather, each is an experience which is thrust upon one or into which one is plunged. In the fullness of time, in proper season according to the creative design of God, the gift and grace of a call to change of heart, to revision of life patterns is sounded from the depths of the soul.

The radical self-communication of God which graces the process of conversion brightens the darkness, dispels the blindness, pierces the deafness, quickens the faltering step, fleshes the heart of stone, redirects the misguided orientation, reorganizes the confusion, orders the chaos and cultivates the desert, laid waste by sin, to blossom as the rose.

The God at work in the process of conversion is the God who enters human life as a restoring artist in the process of mid-life transformation. For those who have eyes to see, ears to hear, and hearts capable of belief, it is one and the same God. Very likely and not surprisingly, it is one and the same process as well.

As the process of conversion evolves toward spiritual integration, the fruits of the transformation are harvested in lived experience. Compassion and commitment are two of the fruits by which conversion is known.

The Gospel imperative "Be perfect as your heavenly Father is perfect" (Matt 5:48) is possibly one of the most misunderstood passages in all of sacred Scripture. Regrettably, the perfection to which Jesus refers is most often interpreted as the cultivation of an attitude of legalistic perfectionism which results in an exaggerated preoccupation with oneself. It encourages an unhealthy emphasis on a type of development which is not only undesireable but well nigh humanly impossible.

A much more humanly attainable, growth-producing perfection toward which to strive is that in which one seeks to be a truly human (and therefore limited) incarnation of the God who is so perfectly and totally loving as to be compassionate. God's total love and complete compassion embraced the human experience from the cradle to the cross. Within a limited life-cycle of thirty-three years, God incarnate so identified with the children of earth as to assume every subtle nuance of thought, feeling, desire, and emotion which fills the mind and heart of a human person. Nothing was foreign, nothing alien except sin. The fullest affirmation of our humanity is revealed in God's refusal to shrink from pain and suffering. In the total embrace of God's yes, even to death by crucifixion, is revealed the meaning of being perfect: being compassionate, being with those whose passion for life enables them to experience joy and sorrow with equal intensity. The God *of* our Lord Jesus Christ, the God who *is* our Lord Jesus Christ is the God who "passions with" us in the slow and painful processes of living, dying, and rising to fuller maturity in the perfection of God's compassion.

The mid-life and conversion processes each lead into and through an experience of weakness, finitude, and limit. They require that one come face-to-face with the reality of the self in all its beauty and brokenness. In tasting one's brokenness, one can become, through compassion, better able to be gentle with the Self even as God is gentle and merciful. Beyond that perfection of compassion which enables the acceptance of the fractured Self is a still more perfected compassion. It is the fruit of meeting one's true Self as a loved sinner before God and before the world that enables one to "passion with" those who are daily touched by the same joys and sorrows, doubts and fears, hopes and dreams that live, die, and are reborn to newness of life and freshness of meaning in the transformative journey in the dark woods of mid-life and conversion. If it be true that the grace of conversion yields perfection and the generativity of mid-life flows into integrity, it may well be that, called by another name, perfection and integrity are none other than compassion.

The third invitation offered by the transformative processes of mid-life and conversion is commitment. As meanings, values, and goals in life are reassessed and rerouted in pursuit of generativity, integrity, and authentic human wholeness, involvements and associations of lesser, even false, worth are abandoned. They are replaced by commitments and dedications now perceived through a new vision. In biblical imagery, idolatry surrenders to true worship.

The realization that time is short and that it grows toward evening is wedded to the awareness that one is yet capable of something but not everything. Choices and decisions, once made with youthful abandon, are now made more carefully and with a more refined discernment. The object of life's energies is now recognized, as never before, as determining the ultimate success or failure of conversion, "middlescence," and the final integration of all life.

Invariably, commitments forged in the crucible of mid-life and conversion emerge purified and intensified as gold tried in the fire. They are characterized by a strength of dedication which transcends human finitude to find ultimate fulfillment in the very Source of Life.

Mid-life and conversion are two symbols which at once reveal and conceal the depth reality of a transformative process which, if one is faithful, leads through generativity to that human integrity which is a commitment to compassion. It is the pilgrim engaged on this perilous journey through desert and dark wood whom the Christian community gathers to support in the alternative ritual of anointing here proposed.

The Ritual

ENVIRONMENT

The theme of this ritual lends itself well to the use of visual symbols. These may be arranged artistically on a table draped with colorful cloth to create a meditative focal point for the celebration. If the space is flexible enough, a circular seating arrangement is preferable, with the table, the symbol station forming part of the circle's circumference. With such an arrangement, the symbol station becomes a point of departure and of closure for the circle, itself an appropriate symbol for mid-life prayer. If the space is not flexible, however, the symbol station should be placed in the foreground where it will be visible to the entire assembly.

The symbols are chosen to be suggestive of the passage and the promise of the mid-life journey. They might include some of the following: a vase containing bittersweet or some other autumn foliage; a large, attractive clock, preferably in a wooden case; a small pillow on which is placed a pair of leather sandals; a roughly hewn walking staff; a partially opened road map; a cluster of medium-sized stones; a pillar candle; a compass; a wooden cross without a corpus. Other symbols might be chosen instead.

Care should be exercised to ensure a harmonious coordination of size and color among all the elements of the symbol station. The point is to provide a contemplative focal point to feed and nourish reflective prayer.

Introductory Rites

GATHERING

As the assembly gathers, soft instrumental music may be played in the background. When everyone is gathered and seated, the presider and attending ministers enter the assembly and take their assigned places. After a brief time of quiet, one of the ministers lights a candle on the symbol table.

CALL TO WORSHIP

Presider: My brothers and sisters in Christ, welcome!

Our lives are filled with turning points,
cycles of change and crisis and transformation.
The old passes into ever new beginnings.
We grow, we stand still, we grow again.

As Christians we believe and proclaim
that God's love is always at work within us,

in men and women who believe and trust and hope.

I welcome you now to this time of prayer,
this time to know again the action of God in our
    lives.
I welcome you to celebrate together
time passing, and time beginning anew.

And I pray that the God of Jesus Christ,
who is ever old and ever new
be with us.

All: As it was in the beginning,
is now and ever shall be,
world without end. Amen.

Liturgy of the Word

MEDITATION

A reader steps to the center of the circle and faces the symbol station. At specified points during the reading of the meditation, the
reader turns to the right in a clockwise movement and faces another
segment of the assembly. The movement is designed to come full
circle when the meditation comes to an end. The reading should be
done slowly and with feeling. Eye contact with the assembly is essential.

Time
turns
taking us
where we would not choose to go.

Reader turns to the right.

Suddenly we pass a point
we will never pass again.
Turning points interrupt us—
there must be some mistake.

Reader turns to the right again.

Looking back we see them
for what they really are:
bittersweet raw reality,
breakthrough to beatitude,
bedrock that gives us courage.

Reader turns to the right again.

> to give ourselves away.
> The less we struggle with turning points
> the greater the strength remaining
> to return

Reader turns again, thus coming full circle.

> and turn
> again.[8]

SONG

The assembly is invited to a sung prayer of hope and trust. A text employing the imagery of journey would be ideal.

PRAYER

Presider: Let us pray.

God of our past, our present, and our future,
we know that we do not travel alone,
for you are with us and within us.
You are the God of seasons and sojourns,
of passage and pilgrimage,
of Exodus and Emmaus.

Be companion with us all the days of our lives.
Direct our steps along the path of goodness and
    growth.
Be gentle with us through the seasons and the years.
Give us power to serve others
in compassion, mercy and love.

Be for us always a new beginning,
a fresh springtime,
and lead us to your eternal day
with him who is the Rising Dawn,
Jesus Christ, our Lord.

All: Amen.

READING: Rom 8:18-27

RESPONSE (based on Eccl 3:1-11)

R℣. For everything there is a season,
    and a time for every purpose under heaven.

A time for new life; a time for mid-life.
A time to begin; a time to make an end.

A time for youth; a time for growing old.
A time for first adventures; a time for second
    journeys. R̈.

A time for growth; a time for standing still.
A time for change; a time to remain the same.
A time for confusion; a time to be well ordered.
A time for fear; a time to trust. R̈.

A time to doubt; a time to be certain.
A time for crisis; a time to be stable.
A time to lose meaning; a time to find it anew.
A time to be weak; a time to be strong. R̈.

A time to face limits; a time to open possibilities.
A time for isolation; a time to be intimate.
A time for alienation; a time to be reconciled.
A time to be alone; a time to be with companions. R̈.

A time for struggle; a time to surrender.
A time to deny death; a time to affirm life.
A time to reject finitude; a time to affirm Infinity.
A time to be mortal; a time to live forever. R̈.

READING: John 21:18-19

HOMILY

The homilist may wish to share reflections on the theme of mid-life journeying and on the importance of responding to Christ's invitation, "Follow me." It is strongly recommended that the homilist be a person who has personal experience of the mid-life transition.

Rite of Anointing

PRESENTATION OF OIL

The presentation is made within the context of a meditative reading which may be rendered by a solo voice or by several voices in dialogue.

> I said to my soul, be still and let the dark come
>   upon you
> Which shall be the darkness of God.

All lights in the worship space are extinguished except for the single candle on the symbol station.

> I said to my soul, be still, and wait without hope,

For hope would be hope for the wrong things;
 wait without love
For love would be love of the wrong thing; there
 is yet faith
But the faith and the love and the hope are all
 in the waiting.

Wait without thought, for you are not ready for
 thought:
So the darkness shall be the light, and the
 stillness, the dancing.

Here the reader pauses long enough to create the sensation of "waiting in darkness."

What we call the beginning is often the end
And to make an end is to make a beginning.
The end is where we start from.

At this point instrumental music is introduced as background accompaniment to the reading. A solo flute or oboe would serve best.

Time present and time past
Are both perhaps present in time future . . . .
What might have been and what has been
Point to one end, which is always present.

At the still point of the turning world . . .
Neither from nor towards; at the still point, there the
 dance is . . . .
Where past and future are gathered . . . .
Except for the point, the still point,
There would be no dance.[9]

The reading and the music cease simultaneously. There is a brief
reflective silence, a still point, before the music resumes. When it
does, a minister enters carrying a decanter of oil for the anointing.
This ritual action may be a simple processional gesture with the
decanter of oil held high, or, if a dancer can be enlisted for this,
it may be a more complex dance presentation. The lights are raised
as the minister or dancer enters the assembly. The oil is presented
to the presider for the blessing.

BLESSING OF OIL

Presider: Blest be God who has given us healing ointments
          with which to salve the wounds and hurts of life.

Blest be this golden liquid,
pressed from the fruits of the earth
and possessed of powers
to nurture healing and wholeness.

Blest be God whose life-giving Spirit
animates the flowing motion
and the fluid ministrations
of this holy unction.

Blest be God who invites us to receive
the healing touch of divine compassion
in the sacrament of anointing.

Blest too be men and women of faith
who respond to God's invitation.

All: Amen.

Oil is poured into several earthenware bowls set aside for the purpose and are given to those who will administer the anointing. These proceed to designated stations.

ANOINTING WITH OIL

The minister signs the head of each person with oil, saying one of the following prayers:

May your journey through mid-life
bring you to fuller maturity in Christ.

[*or:*]   Through this holy anointing,
may you realize more fully
your true humanity in God.

R⁊. Amen.

PRAYER AFTER ANOINTING

When all have been anointed, a prayer of thanksgiving may be offered, or a song sung, or simply some time given to quiet prayer.

Concluding Rites

CLOSING PRAYER

Presider: Let us now pray.

All: From God's infinite glory
may our hidden selves grow strong,
and may Christ live in our hearts through faith.

Then, planted in love and built on love,
we will, with all the saints,
have the strength to grasp
the breadth and the length,
the height and the depth,
until knowing the love of Christ
which is beyond all understanding,
we are filled with the utter fullness of God.

Glory be to God
whose power at work within us
can do infinitely more than we can ask or imagine.
Glory be to God from generation to generation
in the church and in Christ Jesus
forever and ever. Amen.

DISMISSAL

Presider: And so, my friends and fellow voyagers,
I make but one suggestion:
Think not today that the past is finished,
nor even that the future is before us.
Rather, consider the future and the past
with equal mind.

With God's blessing upon us all,
I bid you not "Farewell,"
but "Fare forward."[10]

RECESSIONAL

The solo instrumental recapitulates the theme introduced during the rite of anointing. The minister/dancer re-enters to beckon the presider and the members of the assembly to follow his/her lead in exiting the worship space. As the community departs, the lights are gradually extinguished until the place of prayer is once again in dark stillness. The music continues for a bit after all have departed. Finally, it ceases. All is stillness.

Commentary

The ritual presented here employs a large range of symbol, gesture and movement. This was a deliberate choice. We wanted to include somewhere in this volume a ritual text that incorporates, and thereby illustrates the use of, contributions from the arts. It is probably true that this ritual contains much more than the average assembly might be able to actualize. However, the aim of this whole series is to imagine rituals into being, and to illustrate thereby just how rituals may be imagined into being.

But the deeper reason for the particular shape of this ritual is not finally to offer illustration. The very challenge of the mid-life experience to enter deeply into one's own life, to journey inward rather than outward, invites a style of prayer that is contemplative and evocative. I have attempted to structure a contemplative and evocative event of prayer. It is toward *that* end that I have chosen to include a wide range of suggestive symbols, a good deal of reflective silence, and the evocative language of dance, instrumental music, and body gesture. Should the ritual need to be scaled down, the prayer, the Scripture, the blessing of the oil, and the anointing itself can be lifted out and otherwise appropriately enacted.

A primary reason for both the ritual and the accompanying essay has been to explore the developmental phenomenon of mid-life transition. More importantly, it has been to show good cause from a psychological and theological perspective for including persons in mid-life and others sustaining the collapse of their meaning world in the Church's sacramental ministry of healing through anointing. The intention has been to encourage an expansion of sacramental ritual by offering a creative model for alternative futures for worship which addresses these and other transformative experiences. Hopefully, this has been accomplished and hopefully, too, the Church as the community of God's people on pilgrimage will be open, receptive, and creatively responsive to such alternative futures. It is the dream of the authors of this series that many will be inspired to "wonder" yet other alternative futures into the reality of the Church's present. My prayer is that this work will enable you, the reader, and those to whom you minister to experience more and more fully the mystery of God in your personal and liturgical lives. My faith is that the more you experience God within and beyond liturgical rituals the more too will you experience conversion, compassion, and commitment in all of life. Fareforward.

Footnotes

1. Johannes B. Metz, *Poverty of Spirit* (New York: Paulist, 1978) 19.

2. T. Gerard Connolly, "Spiritual Direction" (Baltimore: Loyola College, 1983), unpublished lecture notes.

3. Gerald O'Collins, *The Second Journey: Spiritual Awareness and the Mid-Life Crisis* (New York: Paulist, 1978).

4. Connolly.

5. William F. Kraft, *Achieving Promises: A Spiritual Guide for the Transitions of Life* (Philadelphia: Westminster, 1981) 60–61.

6. See Gail Sheehy, *Passages* (New York: Dutton, 1977) 5.

7. O'Collins, 68–69.

8. Miriam Therese Winter, *God-with-us* (Nashville: Abingdon, 1979) 35.

9. Selected verses from T. S. Eliot, *The Four Quartets*, in *The Complete Poems and Plays* (New York: Harcourt Brace Jovanovich, 1971) 117–145.

10. *Ibid* 134.

ALTERNATIVE 4: *LITURGY OF HEALING TO REPLACE THE BLESSING OF THROATS FOR THE FEAST OF ST. BLAISE*

Walter H. Cuenin and Peter E. Fink, S.J.

The anointing of the sick is what might be called an "occasional" sacrament, occasioned, of course, by the reality of sickness when and as it inflicts itself upon members of the community. Other rituals in this volume address in a variety of ways what Orlo Strunk, in his opening human sciences essay, has named the personal equation, the text, the specifics of "this person" and "this family" and "this sickness." This final ritual aims to complement the others and respond to the equally important challenge from both the human sciences and the pastoral theology of sacraments, namely, the context in which the sacrament is enacted.

One of the difficulties with "occasional" sacraments is that they are in fact occasional. In the case of the anointing of the sick, the healing ministry of Christ is sacramentally set in motion when sickness arises. Only then is it brought into the domain of the sick person where the sickness itself, and the immediate system of family, friends, and medical personnel provide the primary context for its enactment. Separated as it is from the ordinary patterns of prayer in the community, it can come, as it were, "out of the blue" and be shaped, therefore, only by the attending nuances of the darkness of sickness alone. On days when all is well, the healing ministry of Christ is all but "out of sight" of the prayer and faith of the believing community. Its context is severely restricted and tends to foster, rather than counter, the very isolation it is intended to overcome.

The sacrament of the anointing, as is true of all sacraments, is an act of remembrance. Part of the power of the sacrament lies in what it evokes for those who are sick and for those in immediate attendance upon the sick. If the truth of this sacrament is not in some way kept alive in the ordinary patterns of prayer of a community, and if the hopes and expectations of this sacrament are not formed by the ordinary patterns of prayer of a community, then the ministers of the sacrament as well as the recipients of the Church's ministry will approach the experience of sickness with a ritual act that is impoverished and deprived of its full hope and promise. Occasional sacraments that call upon the faith of the Church for their effectiveness require that that same faith be kept alive when sickness is only a human threat, and not an immediate reality, "lest we forget." In other words, it is an important part of the sacrament of the anointing that its context be established for and within the whole believing community so that when sickness does arise those associated with the sick and the sick themselves will remember and have a rich context to draw on for confidence and hope.

One phenomenon that is already beginning to develop in some places is the commissioning of ministers to the sick at the end of the principal Sunday Eucharistic service. This can serve to illustrate the question of context that is being raised and addressed here. Week after week people in the Sunday assembly see women and men sent forth with the Eucharist to those who for a variety of reasons, usually sickness, are unable to attend. It is the visible link between the faith, love, and prayer of this assembly and those who are absent. It provides a context for all who are gathered so that, should the occasion of sickness arise, and should a minister of the Eucharist come to them, they will know from whence these ministers have come, and remember the love, the faith, the prayer, and the support that these ministers bring with them. How much richer this is than the more familiar situation of the minister showing up, as if from nowhere, to "bring Communion" to the sick.

At the heart of the sacrament of the anointing is the belief that communion with Christ in the church enables the sick person and those around the sick to entrust the sickness to a compassionate and caring God, to offer the sickness as an act of worship whether or not physical healing will be given, and in that offering and entrustment to God to find meaning and peace. Resources for this pro-

found act of worship do not serve well if they are hidden until they
are absolutely necessary. This kind of worship and acceptance does
not come easily. It needs to be formed slowly, and in untroubled
circumstances, if it is to be available when it is most powerfully
needed. The context for the sacrament is essential.

The alternative future offered in this final ritual selection is intended to address this question of context. It is intended for the well
in order to train them in faith for a sickness that may lie ahead.
It is an untroubled ritual for untroubled times, inviting people to
enact, as ordinary fare in their ordinary prayer life, the same faith
and hope and confidence that lies behind the sacrament of the anointing of the sick, namely, in a God who cares, with a Christ who
can heal, among a people who trust and support. It is intended to
keep alive among the well the healing ministry of Christ, "lest we
forget." For if we forget this profound truth of our faith, it will be,
if at all, but a slight whisper and a faint memory when we need
its resources most profoundly. Doctrine may speak this memory
to our minds, but more than doctrine is needed. We need to hear
it with more than our minds. Liturgy trains us in our faith in mind
and heart and in our whole person. It is liturgical act more than
doctrine that will shape the context we need.

Why St. Blaise? The traditional blessing of throats is an act that
is familiar to people, and thus provides an excellent point of departure for the evolution of new forms which, the Constitution on the
Sacred Liturgy advises, should "in some way grow organically from
forms already existing" (CSL 23). Moreover, the blessing of throats
has proven to have a peculiar power even where people have no
particular devotion to St. Blaise, are concerned with more than "illness of the throat," and/or imagine themselves too sophisticated
to partake in such a ritual act. I have myself described this odd power
of the blessing of throats this way: "I sit in the pew thinking of ten
reasons for not getting my throat blessed, and I rehearse in my mind
the last five as I am walking down the aisle for the blessing." In
the odd ways of ritual evolution, St. Blaise is probably the best place
to begin for the context we seek.

February 3 has traditionally been observed in the Catholic
Church with the blessing of the throats in honor of St. Blaise. The
roots of this tradition are somewhat obscure. Blaise was a fourth-
century bishop who died for the faith in Armenia. According to
tradition he cured a boy who was choking on a fish bone. By the
sixth century he was the patron in the East of all those who had

diseases of the throat. He became equally popular in the Western Churches by the ninth century. The custom of blessing throats with candles probably dates from the seventeenth century, and it has been popular ever since. It is not unknown that people who do not normally participate in church services will bring their children on this day for the blessing of throats.

While this traditional custom is popular, it has also provoked some misgivings. Some criticize it because it seems "magical." Others find it strange that, of all the parts of the body, we bless the throat instead, say, of the eyes which are usually considered more important and subject to disease. Some wonder about the liturgical setting of this throat blessing. It is usually done at the end of the mass without any reading from Scripture or other ritual accompaniment. It can thus appear to be dislocated from any serious context of meaning.

In order to attend to some of these concerns and yet to capture seriously the popularity of this blessing, the following ritual form was developed. Its intention is to weave a popular ritual act more deeply into the prayer patterns of the Church community and thus allow it to bring to expression in the lives of believers deep faith and trust in the healing power of God in Christ. As such it can help provide the context for the more specific enactment of that healing power in the sacrament of the anointing when serious illness does indeed arise.

Liturgy of Healing and Blessing

On the Sunday closest to February 3, which is usually a Sunday in Ordinary Time, the parish community celebrates a liturgy of healing. It is a regular Sunday Mass. The readings are chosen from the Mass for the Sick. The prayers are also taken from the Mass for the Sick, but they are adapted in such a way that they focus on all in the assembly and on our common need for the healing power of God.

The traditional blessing of throats is given an expanded meaning in the context of this liturgy. It becomes a symbol of prayer for the healing of the whole body. The ritual gesture of the candles placed around the neck is maintained since it is familiar, but the prayer is changed to express the hope of healing on a deeper level. Additional ministers may assist the presider in giving the blessing.

Introductory Rite

The Eucharist celebration begins in the usual way. For the penitential rite, Form C viii from the Roman *Sacramentary* is suggested.

OPENING PRAYER

> All-powerful and ever-living God,
> the lasting health of all who believe in you,
> hear us as we ask your loving help
> for ourselves and for all who are sick.
>
> Continue to keep us in health of mind and body,
> and grant us your healing mercy
> in whatever way we most deeply are in need.
>
> Keep alive in us a deep trust in your care
> that we may always come to you in confidence
> whether we be well or afflicted with illness.
>
> May we always give you thanks and praise
> through Jesus Christ, our Lord.
>
> Amen.

(Adapted from the alternative opening prayer,
"Mass for the Sick", in the Roman *Sacramentary*)

Liturgy of the Word

The numbers in parentheses refer to the Roman *Lectionary for Mass*.

OLD TESTAMENT READING: (871)

> 2 Kgs 20:1-6 [or]
> Isa 53:1-5, 10-11

RESPONSORIAL PSALM: (873)

NEW TESTAMENT READING: (872)

> Acts 28:7-10 [or]
> 2 Cor 4:10-18 [or]
> 2 Cor 12:7-10 [or]
> Jas 5:13-16

GOSPEL VERSE: (874)

GOSPEL: (875)

> Matt 8:14-17 [or]
> Mark 16:15-20 [or]
> Luke 22:39-43 [or]
> John 15:1-9

Homily

The homily should stress faith and confidence in the healing power of God in Christ.

Rite of Blessing

The people are invited to come forward in silence for the traditional blessing with candles. They are asked to pray in the quiet of their hearts for whatever healing they require in their lives, including the healing of their bodies and also of wounds that are more emotional in nature.

As the following prayer is prayed, the minister places the candles around the throat with one hand and places the other hand on the head of the person being blessed.

Minister: May you know and trust the healing power
of our Lord Jesus Christ.

Recipient: Amen.

During the blessing rite, the choir may sing a hymn or song whose theme is the healing power of God in Christ, or instrumental music may be played.

After all have been blessed:

Presider: Lord Jesus Christ,
you shared our human nature
to heal the sick and save all humankind.
Mercifully listen to our prayers
for our own physical and spiritual health and
well-being.

As we have been blessed in your name,
protect and strengthen us.
May we always hold on to the hope that you give us
in health, in sickness, and in death.

We pray this with confidence
for you are Lord for ever and ever.

All: Amen.

(Adapted from *Pastoral Care of the Sick* #77)

Prayer over the Gifts

God our Father,
your love guides every moment of our lives.
Accept the prayers and the gifts we offer

for our continued health and well-being,
and for a deepened trust in your healing power in
our lives.
We ask this in the name of Jesus the Lord.
Amen.

(Adapted from "Mass for the Sick" in the Roman Sacramentary)

PRAYER AFTER COMMUNION

God our Father,
our help in human weakness,
show forth your healing power ever among us
and keep us in your loving care.

In your kindness and compassion
keep us well in body, mind and heart.
And when we fall ill,
give us your healing and peace.

We ask this through Christ our Lord.
Amen.

(Adapted from "Mass for the Sick" in the Roman Sacramentary)

Index